Anonymous

Epworth Hymnal No. 2

Containing standard Hymns of the Church, Songs for the Sunday-School, etc.

Anonymous

Epworth Hymnal No. 2
Containing standard Hymns of the Church, Songs for the Sunday-School, etc.

ISBN/EAN: 9783337181185

Printed in Europe, USA, Canada, Australia, Japan

Cover: Foto ©Thomas Meinert / pixelio.de

More available books at **www.hansebooks.com**

THE
EPWORTH HYMNAL
No. 2.

CONTAINING

STANDARD HYMNS OF THE CHURCH

SONGS FOR THE SUNDAY-SCHOOL

SONGS FOR SOCIAL SERVICES

SONGS FOR YOUNG PEOPLE'S SOCIETIES

SONGS FOR THE HOME CIRCLE

SONGS FOR SPECIAL OCCASIONS

NEW YORK: HUNT & EATON

CINCINNATI: CRANSTON & STOWE

Copyright, 1891 by HUNT & EATON, New York

EXTRACT FROM THE PREFACE OF EPWORTH HYMNAL NO. 1.

IN the old parish of Epworth, in Lincolnshire, England, lived the earnest, eccentric, and scholarly father, and the gifted, wise, and consecrated mother, of the illustrious John and Charles Wesley.

The story of Samuel Wesley's ministry at Epworth, extending over a period of thirty-nine years—from 1696 to 1735—is alive with interest. The people whom he served were, for the most part, poor, ignorant, coarse, and cruel. Those were days of political strife, when missiles and firebrands were used as arguments. The godly rector, unflinching in his devotion to conviction, paid the price of his fidelity.

In poverty most oppressive, in conflicts most bitter, in labors most abundant, did the old rectory of Epworth hold and train the remarkable family from which were to come forth two of the most widely known and most successful workers in the Church of God—the one a preacher and bishop, the other a writer of sacred hymns. By sermon and song they two went forth to make known to the world the exceeding glory and the saving power of the Lord Jesus; to defend by Scripture the great doctrines of redemption, and by persuasive song to win the hearts of men from sin to righteousness, from self to Christ.

However grand the work and its results, we must not forget that the beginnings and the most valuable preparations were at Epworth, where Samuel Wesley studied and prayed and served, and where Susannah Wesley trained her children, counseled her husband, instructed their parishioners, and walked with God. Before Oxford was Epworth. Before Bristol and City Road Chapel was Epworth.

The poetic fire burned in Samuel Wesley. It reached white heat in the soul of his son Charles, "who was a poet by nature and habit," and of whose productions a distinguished critic says: "There are no hymns in the world of such 'spontaneous devotion,' none so loftily spiritual, none so unmistakably genuine and intensely earnest, as the best-known and largely used of Wesley's."*

John Wesley was also a writer of hymns, a lover of poetry, and a firm believer in the service of song as a means of grace for saints, and of awakening for sinners. He urged all the people to sing. He gave wise directions concerning the spirit and manner of singing, and his followers in all parts of the world have been famous for the ardor and power with which they have sung the praises of the Lord.

All this carries us back to Epworth, where, in addition to the songs of the rectory at family worship, we hear from the church the songs of the people as the faithful rector taught them to sing. The biographer of "The Mother of the Wesleys" says: "Samuel Wesley regarded psalmody as 'the most elevated part of public worship.' Notwithstanding his love for 'anthems and cathedral music,' he was willing to forego his own preferences for the sake of his uneducated flock, and allowed 'the novel way of parochial singing.' . . . Discarding the lazy and inharmonious drawlings of a choir of ignorant and self-important rustics, he resolutely set himself to teach the congregation and children the divine art of sacred song. His efforts were so successful that he declares 'they did sing well after it had cost a pretty deal to teach them.'"

Thus from the Epworth church and parsonage rang out strains of music that have attracted the attention of the world; filled chapel, cathedral, and tented grove with melody; lifted the cry of penitence and the shout of triumph to the heavens; filled the mouths of children with praise, the hearts of believers with joy, the chamber of death with the pæans of victory.

The Committee appointed in pursuance of the action of the General Conference to prepare this book has done well in calling it the THE EPWORTH HYMNAL. Besides a certain euphony in the title, there come with it reverent and grateful thoughts concerning the character and services of the most excellent father of the Wesleys, and that modern Monica, whose strength and loveliness, whose piety and scholarship, are so manifest in the sons whom generations honor. There come also with the title—THE EPWORTH HYMNAL—memories of family prayer and family songs, of neighbors gathered by the devout Susannah on Sunday afternoons for special services of prayer, praise, and admonition, and of the meetings in Epworth church for the training of all the people, old and young, to sing the songs of the sanctuary.

* * * * * * * * *

Sweet home of Epworth, where reverent scholarship presided; where parents governed and children obeyed; where the Holy Scriptures were continually quoted and habitually followed;

---

* The Rev. Frederic M. Bird in *Bibliotheca Sacra*. 1864.

PREFACE.

where songs rose from grateful hearts to the listening heavens; where the voice of prayer was scarcely ever silent; where neighbors were collected for worship and counsel; where each child was brought into sacred conference with its mother concerning the soul, the law of God, the grace of Christ, and the home in heaven!

May our homes be full of law and liberty, of grace and gladness; and from them may there come into Sunday-school, social meeting, and public service those who are well prepared to study the word of God diligently, pray reverently, sing heartily, listen attentively, and live consistently!

J. H. VINCENT.

PREFACE TO THE EPWORTH HYMNAL NO. 2.

THE EPWORTH HYMNAL, introduced to the Church in the stirring words repeated above, was received with a welcome worthy of its merits. After six years of faithful service, and of abounding popularity, there arose a demand for its revision. It was decided by the Committee, in consultation with the Book Agents, that the original work should be left unchanged, and that EPWORTH HYMNAL No. 2, upon the same plan, should be prepared.

The Committee in the compilation of this work consisted of the following: Mr. JAMES M'GEE, Chairman; Mr. A. S. NEWMAN, Musical Editor; the Rev. JAMES S. CHADWICK, D.D., and the Rev. JESSE L. HURLBUT, D.D. To the industry, the judgment, and the taste of the musical editor the merits of the book are largely due. He has been assisted in the details of arrangement by Mr. S. V. R. Ford, musical editor of the Methodist Book Concern. The Responsive Services were prepared for this work by the Rev. J. E. Price, D.D., of New York.

Special thanks should be rendered to Drs. H. R. Palmer and George W. Warren, Mrs. Joseph F. Knapp, Messrs. Walter R. Johnston, Robert L. Fletcher, S. F. Ackley, William J. Kirkpatrick, Theodore E. Perkins, Charles H. Gabriel, F. L. Armstrong, and others for their kindness in permitting the use of their musical compositions.

Since the first hymnal of this name appeared the word "Epworth" has received additional import in the establishment of the Epworth League, which has called forth the activities of the young people. For the chapters of this great organization, and for the needs of other young people's societies, a special department of this work has been added. We trust that these songs will be received with favor and sung with enthusiasm by all our young people.

We present this work to the constituency of its predecessor with the hope that in the social services of the church, in the young people's devotional meeting, and in the Sunday-school it may aid us all to sing with the spirit, and with the understanding also.

New York, July 25, 1891.   JESSE L. HURLBUT.

RESPONSIVE SERVICES

FOR THE

Sunday-School and Social Meetings.

OPENING SERVICE FOR THE SUNDAY-SCHOOL.

Leader. O come, let us worship and bow down :
School. Let us kneel before the Lord, our maker.
L. For the Lord is a great God.
S. And a great King above all gods.
L. In his hands are all the corners of the earth.
S The strength of the hills is his also.
L. He is the Lord our God.
S. And we are the people of his pasture, and the sheep of his hand.
L. O worship the Lord in the beauty of holiness.
S. Let the whole earth stand in awe of him.
L. The law of the Lord is perfect, converting the soul.
S. The testimony of the Lord is sure, making wise the simple.
L. The statutes of the Lord are right, rejoicing the heart: the commandment of the Lord is pure, enlightening the eyes.
S. The fear of the Lord is clean, enduring forever: the judgments of the Lord are true and righteous altogether.
L. More to be desired are they than gold, yea, than much fine gold :
S. Sweeter also than honey and the honeycomb.
L. Moreover by them is thy servant warned :
S. And in keeping of them there is great reward.
All. Let the words of my mouth, and the meditation of my heart, be acceptable in thy sight, O Lord, my strength, and my redeemer.
Singing. Awake, My Soul. No. 6.
PRAYER.

CLOSING SERVICE.

Leader. All Scripture is given by inspiration of God,
School. And is profitable for doctrine, for reproof, for correction, for instruction in righteousness.
L. The grass withereth, the flower fadeth: but the word of our God shall stand forever.
S. Blessed are they that hear the word of God and keep it.
All. Blessed are they that do his commandments, that they may have right to the tree of life, and may enter in through the gates into the city.
Singing. A closing hymn.

OPENING SERVICE FOR THE SUNDAY-SCHOOL.

No. 2.

Leader. Praise waiteth for thee, O God, in Zion: and unto thee shall the vow be performed.
School. We will go into his tabernacle, we will worship at his footstool.
L. Thy testimonies are very sure :
S. Holiness becometh thine house, O Lord, forever.
L. But be ye doers of the word, and not hearers only.
S. Teach me thy way, O Lord, and lead me in a plain path.
L. I am the way, the truth, and the life.
S. And thou shalt call his name Jesus ; for he shall save his people from their sins.
L. And he shall live, and to him shall be given of the gold of Sheba :
S. Prayer also shall be made for him continually ; and daily shall he be praised.
L. His name shall endure forever : his name shall be continued as long as the sun.
S. And men shall be blessed in him; all nations shall call him blessed.
L. Blessed be the Lord God, the God of Israel, who only doeth wondrous things.
S. And blessed be his glorious name forever.
All. And let the whole earth be filled with his glory. Amen and Amen.
Singing. What Glory Gilds the Sacred Page. No. 96.
PRAYER.

RESPONSIVE SERVICES.

CLOSING SERVICE.
No. 2.

All. Now the God of peace, that brought again from the dead our Lord Jesus, that great Shepherd of the sheep, through the blood of the everlasting covenant, make you perfect in every good work to do his will, working in you that which is well-pleasing in his sight, through Jesus Christ; to whom be glory for ever and ever. Amen.

OPENING SERVICE FOR THE PRAYER-MEETING.

Leader. O taste and see that the Lord is good: blessed is the man that trusteth in him.
Congregation. His favor is life, and his loving-kindness is better than life.
L. Whom have I in heaven but thee!
C. And who is there in the earth that I desire besides thee!
L. How excellent is thy loving-kindness, O God!
C. Therefore the children of men put their trust under the shadow of thy wing.
Singing. Nearer the Cross. No. 177.
L. If we walk in the light as he is in the light, we have fellowship one with another;
C. And the blood of Jesus Christ his Son cleanseth us from all sin.
L. Purge me with hyssop, and I shall be clean:
C. Wash me, and I shall be whiter than snow.
L. Create in me a clean heart, O God;
C. And renew a right spirit within me.
L. Then will I teach transgressors thy ways;
C. And sinners shall be converted unto thee.
Singing. I Bring My Sins to Thee. No. 98.
L. Seek ye the Lord while he may be found,
C. Call ye upon him while he is near.
L. This poor man cried and the Lord heard him, and delivered him out of all his troubles.
C. The effectual fervent prayer of a righteous man availeth much.
L. Wait on the Lord: be of good courage, and he shall strengthen thine heart:
C. Wait, I say, on the Lord.
L. My God shall supply all your need according to his riches in glory by Christ Jesus.
PRAYER.

OPENING SERVICE FOR THE PRAYER-MEETING.
No. 2.

Leader. This is a faithful saying, and worthy of all acceptation, that Christ Jesus came into the world to save sinners.
Congregation. In whom we have redemption through his blood, even the forgiveness of sins.
L. God commendeth his love toward us, in that, while we were yet sinners, Christ died for us.
C. He loved me and gave himself for me.
L. But of him are ye in Christ Jesus, who of God is made unto us wisdom, and righteousness, and sanctification, and redemption.
Singing. Of Him who Did Salvation Bring. No. 118.
L. Behold, how good and how pleasant it is for brethren to dwell together in unity!
C. Forsake not the assembling of yourselves together.
L. A new commandment I give unto you, that ye love one another.
C. I pray for them: I pray not for the world, but for them which thou hast given me; for they are thine.
L. And all mine are thine, and thine are mine; and I am glorified in them.
C. And now I am no more in the world, but these are in the world, and I come to thee. Holy Father, keep through thine own name those whom thou hast given me, that they may be one, as we are.
L. Neither pray I for these alone, but for them also which shall believe on me through their word;
C. That they all may be one; as thou, Father, art in me, and I in thee, that they also may be one in us: that the world may believe that thou hast sent me.
Singing. Consecration. No. 147.
L. If ye then, being evil, know how to give good gifts unto your children; how much more shall your heavenly Father give the Holy Spirit to them that ask him?
C. Ask, and it shall be given; seek, and ye shall find; knock, and it shall be opened unto you.
L. Come unto me, all ye that labor and are heavy laden, and I will give you rest.
PRAYER.

OPENING SERVICE FOR YOUNG PEOPLE'S MEETINGS.

Leader. It is good to sing praises unto our God; for it is pleasant; and praise is comely.
Congregation. O come, let us sing unto the Lord:
L. Let us make a joyful noise to the Rock of our salvation.
C. Praise ye the Lord from the heavens; praise him in the heights.
L. Both young men, and maidens; old men, and children:
C. Let them praise the name of the Lord
Singing. Sweet is the Work, O Lord. No. 28.
L. How amiable are thy tabernacles, O Lord of hosts!
C. I had rather be a doorkeeper in the house of my God, than to dwell in the tents of wickedness.
L. Out of Zion, the perfection of beauty, God hath shined.

RESPONSIVE SERVICES.

C. Christ also loved the church, and gave himself for it ;
L. That he might sanctify and cleanse it with the washing of water by the word,
C. That he might present it to himself a glorious church, not having spot, or wrinkle, or any such thing; but that it should be holy and without blemish.
L. One thing have I desired of the Lord, that will I seek after,
C. That I may dwell in the house of the Lord all the days of my life, to behold the beauty of the Lord and to inquire in his temple.
Singing. My God, the Spring of all My Joys. No. 180.
L. The Lord is my shepherd ; I shall not want.
C. He maketh me to lie down in green pastures: he leadeth me beside the still waters.
L. I am the good shepherd, and know my sheep, and am known of mine.
C. As the Father knoweth me, even so know I the Father: and I lay down my life for the sheep.
L. When the chief Shepherd shall appear, ye shall receive a crown of glory that fadeth not away.
Singing. Jesus, Saviour, Pilot Me. No. 13.
PRAYER.

OPENING SERVICE FOR YOUNG PEOPLE'S MEETINGS.

No. 2.

Leader. Blessed be the God and Father of our Lord Jesus Christ,
Congregation. Which according to his abundant mercy hath begotten us again unto a lively hope by the resurrection of Jesus Christ from the dead,
L. To an inheritance incorruptible, and undefiled, and that fadeth not away, reserved in heaven for you,
C. Who are kept by the power of God through faith unto salvation ready to be revealed in the last time.
Singing. The Name of Jesus. No. 51.
L. Labor not for the meat which perisheth, but for that meat which endureth unto everlasting life,
C. Which the Son of man shall give unto you.
L. Our fathers did eat manna in the desert; as it is written, He gave them bread from heaven to eat.
C. And Jesus said unto them, I am the bread of life: he that cometh to me shall never hunger.
L. Then said they unto him, Lord, evermore give us this bread.
Singing. All the Way. No. 243.
L. Brethren, if any of you do err from the truth, and one convert him;

C. Let him know, that he which converteth the sinner from the error of his way shall save a soul from death, and hide a multitude of sins.
L. Say not ye, There are four months, and then cometh harvest ? behold, I say unto you, Lift up your eyes, and look on the fields; for they are white already to harvest.
C. And he that reapeth receiveth wages, and gathereth fruit unto life eternal.
L. Therefore, my beloved brethren, be ye steadfast, unmovable, always abounding in the work of the Lord.
C. I must work the works of him that sent me, while it is day: the night cometh, when no man can work.
L. And besides this, giving all diligence, add to your faith virtue; and to virtue, knowledge.
C. For so an entrance shall be ministered unto you abundantly into the everlasting kingdom of our Lord and Saviour Jesus Christ.
Singing. Do Something To-day. No. 198.
PRAYER.

A SERVICE OF PRAISE.

Singing. Praise God, from whom all blessings flow.
Leader. Praise waiteth for thee, O God, in Zion: and unto thee shall the vow be performed.
Congregation. By terrible things in righteousness wilt thou answer us, O God of our salvation;
L. Who art the confidence of all the ends of the earth, and of them that are afar off upon the sea.
C. They also that dwell in the uttermost parts are afraid at thy tokens: thou makest the outgoings of the morning and evening to rejoice.
L. Thou visitest the earth, and waterest it:
C. Thou greatly enrichest it with the river of God, which is full of water:
L. Thou preparest them corn, when thou hast so provided for it.
C. Thou waterest the ridges thereof abundantly: thou settlest the furrows thereof.
L. Thou crownest the year with thy goodness; and thy paths drop fatness.
C. The pastures are clothed with flocks: the valleys also are covered over with corn; they shout for joy, they also sing.
Singing. Lord of the Worlds Above. No. 1.
L. For God so loved the world, that he gave his only begotten Son,
C. That whosoever believeth in him should not perish, but have everlasting life.
L. And the Word was made flesh, and dwelt among us.
C. In him was life; and the life was the light of men.
L. No man hath seen God at any time;
C. The only begotten Son, which is in the bosom of the Father, he hath declared him.

RESPONSIVE SERVICES.

L. God commendeth his love toward us, in that, while we were yet sinners, Christ died for us.
C. Thanks be unto God for his unspeakable gift.
Singing. When Marshaled on the Nightly Plain. No. 52.
L. The wilderness and the solitary place shall be glad for them; and the desert shall rejoice, and blossom as the rose.
C. It shall blossom abundantly, and rejoice even with joy and singing:
L. The glory of Lebanon shall be given unto it, the excellency of Carmel and Sharon;
C. They shall see the glory of the Lord, and the excellency of our God.
L. Then the eyes of the blind shall be opened,
C. And the ears of the deaf shall be unstopped.
L. His name shall be called Wonderful,
C. The mighty God, The everlasting Father, The Prince of Peace.
Singing. At the Lamb's High Feast We Sing. No. 59.
L. I was glad when they said unto me, Let us go into the house of the Lord.
C. Our feet shall stand within thy gates, O Jerusalem.
L. Let us come before his presence with thanksgiving, and make a joyful noise unto him with psalms,
C. For the Lord is a great God, and a great King above all gods.
L. But as for me, I will come into thy house in the multitude of thy mercy: and in thy fear will I worship toward thy holy temple.
C. Lord, I have loved the habitation of thy house, and the place where thine honor dwelleth.
L. Ye that stand in the house of the Lord, in the courts of the house of our God,
C. Praise the Lord; for the Lord is good: sing praises unto his name; for it is pleasant.
L. In Judah is God known; his name is great in Israel. In Salem also is his tabernacle, and his dwelling-place in Zion.
C. For the Lord hath chosen Zion; he hath desired it for his habitation.
L. The Lord loveth the gates of Zion more than all the dwellings of Jacob.
C. Sing praises to the Lord, which dwelleth in Zion: declare among the people his doings.
L. Great is the Lord, and greatly to be praised,
C. In the city of our God, in the mountain of his holiness.
Singing. Within Thy House, O Lord, Our God. No. 2.
L. Make a joyful noise unto God, all ye lands:
C. Sing forth the honor of his name: make his praise glorious.
L. O sing unto the Lord a new song: sing unto the Lord, all the earth.
C. Say among the heathen that the Lord reigneth. Let the multitude of isles be glad thereof.
L. Thus saith the Lord God, Behold, I will lift up mine hand to the Gentiles,
C. And set up my standard to the people.
L. I will bring thy seed from the east,
C. And gather thee from the west:
L. I will say to the north, Give up;
C. And to the south, Keep not back:
L. Bring my sons from far,
C. And my daughters from the ends of the earth.
Singing. Soon May the Last Glad Song Arise. No. 185.
L. And a highway shall be there, and a way, and it shall be called The way of holiness;
C. The unclean shall not pass over it; but it shall be for those: the wayfaring men, though fools, shall not err therein.
L. No lion shall be there, nor any ravenous beast shall go up thereon, it shall not be found there;
C. But the redeemed shall walk there:
L. And the ransomed of the Lord shall return, and come to Zion with songs and everlasting joy upon their heads:
C. They shall obtain joy and gladness, and sorrow and sighing shall flee away.
Singing. Rejoice and be Glad. No. 216.
L. Whom having not seen, ye love; in whom, though now ye see him not, yet believing, ye rejoice with joy unspeakable and full of glory:
C. Receiving the end of your faith, even the salvation of your souls.
L. As many as received him, to them gave he power to become the sons of God.
C. The Spirit himself beareth witness with our spirits that we are the children of God.
Singing. Still, Still with Thee. No. 39.
[Here let there be a call for testimonies of thanksgiving, for which an appropriate topic, such as Daily Benefits, The Goodness of God, The Love of Christ, etc., may be announced.]
PRAYER.
L. O that men would praise the Lord for his goodness,
C. And for his wonderful works to the children of men.
L. The Lord is good to all, and his tender mercies are over all his works.
C. All thy works shall praise thee, O Lord; and thy saints shall bless thee.
Singing. Glory be to God on High. No. 41.
All. Now unto the King eternal, immortal, invisible, the only wise God, be honor and glory for ever and ever. Amen.

A SERVICE WITH THE PROMISES.

Leader. Grace and peace be multiplied unto you through the knowledge of God, and of Jesus our Lord,

RESPONSIVE SERVICES.

Congregation. According as his divine power hath given unto us all things that pertain unto life and godliness, through the knowledge of him that hath called us to glory and virtue:
L. Whereby are given unto us exceeding great and precious promises;
C. That by these ye might be partakers of the divine nature.
Singing. All are Mine. No. 46.
L. The Lord is my light and my salvation; whom shall I fear?
C. The Lord is the strength of my life; of whom shall I be afraid?
L. For in the time of trouble he shall hide me in his pavilion:
C. In the secret of his tabernacle shall he hide me.
L. And the Lord shall guide thee continually:
C. I will instruct thee, and teach thee in the way which thou shalt go; I will guide thee with mine eye.
Singing. The Rock that is Higher than I. No. 139.
L. This poor man cried, and the Lord heard him, and saved him out of all his troubles.
C. The angel of the Lord encampeth round about them that fear him, and delivereth them.
L. O fear the Lord, ye his saints; for there is no want to them that fear him.
C. The steps of a good man are ordered by the Lord; and he delighteth in his way.
L. Thou shalt guide me with thy counsel, and afterward receive me to glory.
C. For this God is our God for ever and ever; he will be our guide even unto death.
Singing. Our Father Watcheth O'er Us. No. 29.
L. My brethren, count it all joy when ye fall into divers temptations;
C. Knowing this, that the trying of your faith worketh patience.
L. There hath no temptation taken you but such as is common to man;
C. But God is faithful, who will not suffer you to be tempted above that ye are able; but will with the temptation also make a way to escape, that ye may be able to bear it.
L. Blessed is the man that endureth temptation:
C. For when he is tried, he shall receive the crown of life.
Singing. Go Tell it to Jesus. No. 150.
L. All things work together for good to them that love God.
C. When thou passest through the waters, I will be with thee; and through the rivers, they shall not overflow thee.
L. Many are the afflictions of the righteous; but the Lord delivereth him out of them all.
C. The eternal God is thy refuge, and underneath are the everlasting arms.

L. Although the fig-tree shall not blossom, neither shall fruit be in the vines:
C. The labor of the olive shall fail, and the fields shall yield no meat;
L. The flock shall be cut off from the fold, and there shall be no herd in the stalls:
C. Yet I will rejoice in the Lord, I will joy in the God of my salvation.
Singing. God's Promises. No. 38.
L. If we say that we have no sin, we deceive ourselves, and the truth is not in us.
C. If we confess our sins, he is faithful and just to forgive us our sins, and to cleanse us from all unrighteousness.
L. And if any man sin, we have an advocate with the Father, Jesus Christ the righteous:
C. And he is the propitiation for our sins: and not for ours only, but also for the sins of the whole world.
Singing. Wondrous Love. No. 77.
L. Let not your heart be troubled: ye believe in God, believe also in me.
C. In my Father's house are many mansions: if it were not so, I would have told you. I go to prepare a place for you.
L. And if I go and prepare a place for you, I will come again, and receive you unto myself; that where I am, there ye may be also.
C. And God shall wipe away all tears from their eyes; and there shall be no more death, neither sorrow, nor crying, neither shall there be any more pain: for the former things are passed away.
Singing. Jerusalem. No. 211.
[Here let all quote a favorite promise, especially a promise tested in personal experience.]
L. But the day of the Lord will come as a thief in the night; in the which the heavens shall pass away with a great noise, and the elements shall melt with fervent heat.
C. Seeing then that all these things shall be dissolved, what manner of persons ought ye to be in all holy conversation and godliness?
L. Nevertheless we, according to his promise, look for new heavens, and a new earth, wherein dwelleth righteousness.
C. Watch therefore: for ye know not what hour your Lord doth come.
L. Blessed are those servants, whom the lord when he cometh shall find watching:
C. Verily I say unto you, that he shall gird himself, and make them to sit down to meat, and will come forth and serve them.
Singing. I am Sheltered in Thee. No. 158.
All. Now unto him that is able to do exceeding abundantly above all that we ask or think, according to the power that worketh in us, unto him be glory in the church by Christ Jesus, throughout all ages, world without end. Amen.

RESPONSIVE SERVICES.

THE BEATITUDES.

Blessed are the poor in spirit: for theirs is the kingdom of heaven.

Blessed are they that mourn: for they shall be comforted.

Blessed are the meek: for they shall inherit the earth.

Blessed are they which do hunger and thirst after righteousness: for they shall be filled.

Blessed are the merciful: for they shall obtain mercy.

Blessed are the pure in heart: for they shall see God.

Blessed are the peace-makers: for they shall be called the children of God.

Blessed are they which are persecuted for righteousness' sake: for theirs is the kingdom of heaven.

Blessed are ye, when men shall revile you, and persecute you, and shall say all manner of evil against you falsely, for my sake.

Rejoice, and be exceeding glad: for great is your reward in heaven: for so persecuted they the prophets which were before you.

THE TEN COMMANDMENTS.

And God spake all these words, saying,

I. Thou shalt have no other gods before me.

II. Thou shalt not make unto thee any graven image, or any likeness of any thing that is in heaven above, or that is in the earth beneath, or that is in the water under the earth: thou shalt not bow down thyself to them, nor serve them: for I the Lord thy God am a jealous God, visiting the iniquity of the fathers upon the children unto the third and fourth generation of them that hate me; and showing mercy unto thousands of them that love me, and keep my commandments.

III. Thou shalt not take the name of the Lord thy God in vain: for the Lord will not hold him guiltless that taketh his name in vain.

IV. Remember the Sabbath-day, to keep it holy. Six days shalt thou labor, and do all thy work: but the seventh day is the Sabbath of the Lord thy God: in it thou shalt not do any work, thou, nor thy son, nor thy daughter, thy man-servant, nor thy maid-servant, nor thy cattle, nor thy stranger that is within thy gates: for in six days the Lord made heaven and earth, the sea, and all that in them is, and rested the seventh day: wherefore the Lord blessed the Sabbath-day, and hallowed it.

V. Honor thy father and thy mother: that thy days may be long upon the land which the Lord thy God giveth thee.

VI. Thou shalt not kill.

VII. Thou shalt not commit adultery.

VIII. Thou shalt not steal.

IX. Thou shalt not bear false witness against thy neighbor.

X. Thou shalt not covet thy neighbor's house, thou shalt not covet thy neighbor's wife, nor his man-servant, nor his maid-servant, nor his ox, nor his ass, nor any thing that is thy neighbor's.

BAPTISMAL COVENANT.

I renounce the devil and all his works, the vain pomp and glory of the world, with all covetous desires of the same, and the carnal desires of the flesh, so that I will not follow nor be led by them.

The Apostles' Creed.

I believe in God the Father Almighty, Maker of heaven and earth; and in Jesus Christ his only Son our Lord; who was conceived by the Holy Ghost, born of the Virgin Mary, suffered under Pontius Pilate; was crucified, dead, and buried; the third day he rose from the dead; he ascended into heaven, and sitteth on the right hand of God the Father Almighty; from thence he shall come to judge the quick and the dead.

I believe in the Holy Ghost; the Holy Catholic Church,* the communion of saints; the forgiveness of sins; the resurrection of the body, and the life everlasting. *Amen.*

Having been baptized in this faith, I will obediently keep God's holy will and commandments, and walk in the same all the days of my life, God being my helper.

---

* By the Holy Catholic Church is meant the Church of God in general.

Order of Arrangement.

	HYMNS
SONGS OF WORSHIP	1–20
SONGS OF THE SABBATH	21–28
SONGS OF GOD	29–43
SONGS OF CHRIST	44–87
SONGS OF THE HOLY SPIRIT	88–91
SONGS OF THE SCRIPTURES	92–96
SONGS OF SALVATION	97–138
SONGS OF THE CHRISTIAN LIFE	139–181
SONGS OF THE CHURCH	182–191
SONGS FOR YOUNG PEOPLE'S SOCIETIES	192–206
SONGS OF HEAVEN	207–216
SONGS FOR THE LITTLE ONES	217–228
SONGS—MISCELLANEOUS	229–253
TOPICAL INDEX ..Page	227
INDEX OF FIRST LINES "	228–232

NOTICE.

All persons are hereby cautioned against printing any of the copyrighted hymns or tunes contained in this book without the written consent of the owners of copyright.

THE EPWORTH HYMNAL.
No. 2.

LORD OF THE WORLDS ABOVE.   S. V. R. Ford.

1. Lord of the worlds a-bove, How pleasant and how fair The dwellings of thy love, . . . Thy earth-ly tem-ples are! To thine a-bode My heart as-pires, With warm de-sires To see my God.

Copyright, 1891, by Hunt & Eaton.

2 O happy souls, that pray
  Where God appoints to hear!
  O happy men, that pay
    Their constant service there!
They praise thee still: | That love the way,
And happy they | To Zion's hill.

3 They go from strength to strength
  Through this dark vale of tears,
  Till each arrives at length,
    Till each in heaven appears;
O glorious seat; | Shall thither bring
When God our King, | Our willing feet.
                            Isaac Watts.

SONGS OF WORSHIP.

BELMONT. C. M. — SAMUEL WEBBE.

1. Within thy house, O Lord our God In majesty appear;
Make this a place of thine abode, And shed thy blessings here.

2
Invoking divine blessings.

2 As we thy mercy-seat surround,
  Thy Spirit, Lord, impart;
And let thy gospel's joyful sound,
  With power reach every heart.

3 Here let the blind their sight obtain;
  Here give the mourner rest;

Let Jesus here triumphant reign,
  Enthroned in every breast.

4 Here let the voice of sacred joy
  And fervent prayer arise,
Till higher strains our tongues employ,
  In realms beyond the skies.
                    Unknown.

LIGHT OF LIFE. — DYKES.

1. Light of life, seraphic fire, Love divine, thyself impart:
Every fainting soul inspire, Shine in ev'ry drooping heart;

3

2 Every mournful sinner cheer,
    Scatter all our guilty gloom;
  Son of God, appear, appear!
    To thy human temples come.

3 Come in this accepted hour;
    Bring thy heavenly kingdom in;

Fill us with thy glorious power,
  Rooting out the seeds of sin:

4 Nothing more can we require,
    We will covet nothing less;
  Be thou all our heart's desire,
    All our joy, and all our peace.
                    Charles Wesley.

SONGS OF WORSHIP.

THE PLACE OF PRAYER. Robert L. Fletcher.

1. How sweet the place of pray'r, Where kindred spirits meet; From ev-'ry earthly care, How pre-cious a re-treat: Be-fore the throne of grace, Our of-fer-ings we bring, And worship on-ly thee, Our Saviour, Priest and King. How sweet the place of pray'r! How sweet the place of pray'r! Each time more precious seems The hallow'd place of pray'r.

Used by per. of Robert L. Fletcher, owner of Copyright.

2 Here, at the place of prayer,
   So near to thee, and heaven,
 Dear Lord, thyself reveal,
   And speak our sins forgiven:
 And, free from conscious guilt,
   We'll own thy matchless grace,
 Till prayer shall end in praise,
   When we behold thy face.

3 How sweet the place of prayer,
   With grateful memories crowned;
 How sweet to linger near,
   Where living streams abound;
 Oh, sacred trysting place,
   For Jesus meets us here;
 Each waiting soul to bless,
   That feels his presence near.

R. L. F.

SONGS OF WORSHIP.

SING HIS PRAISE.—*Concluded.*

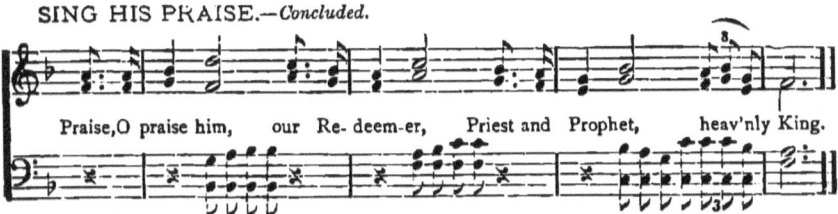

5
2 Children in the temple praised him,
  Sang hosannas to his name;
Shall not we who know his favor
  Tell abroad his wondrous fame?
Angels, too, with harps and voices,
  Loud their notes of rapture raise;
How much more shall we, his children,
  Spread his glory, sing his praise!

3 Every star that shines above us
  Adds a lustre to his fame;
Every flower that blooms around us
  Yields a fragrance to his name;
All the heavenly host adore him
  On the bright, eternal shore;
There, with them our voices blending,
  We shall praise him evermore.
                    Robert L. Fletcher, by per.

AWAKE MY SOUL. L. M.

6
2 He saw me ruined in the fall,
  Yet loved me notwithstanding all;
  He saved me from my lost estate,
  His loving-kindness, oh, how great!

3 Though numerous hosts of mighty foes,
  Though earth and hell my way oppose,
  He safely leads my soul along,
  His loving-kindness, oh, how strong!

SONGS OF WORSHIP.

HEAVENLY FATHER GRANT THY BLESSING.
L. Wilder.

7

2 What a boon to us is given,
   Thus to lift our voice on high,
Well assured the ear of heaven
   Hears our wants, and will supply.
Weak and sinful, oh how often,
   Must we look to God alone,
For his grace our hearts to soften,
   And sustain us as his own!

3 Bless, O Lord, this happy meeting,
   While we stay, and when we go:
Here our hearts in friendly greeting,
   Gladly join thy praise below;
But all earthly unions sever,
   All their pleasures quickly fly:
Oh for grace to praise thee ever,
   In that better world on high.
                     L. Wilder.

SONGS OF WORSHIP.

THE SHADOWS OF THE EVENING HOURS.　　　H. HILES.

1. The shadows of the evening hours Fall from the dark'ning sky,
Upon the fragrance of the flow'rs The dews of evening lie;
Before thy throne, O Lord of heav'n! We kneel at close of day;
Look on thy children from on high, And hear us while we pray.

8

2 The sorrows of thy servants, Lord,
　Oh, do not thou despise,
But let the incense of our prayers
　Before thy mercy rise;
The brightness of the coming night
　Upon the darkness rolls;
With hopes of future glory chase
　The shadows from our souls.
3 Slowly the rays of daylight fade;
　So fade within our heart
The hopes in earthly love and joy,
　That one by one depart;

Slowly the bright stars, one by one,
　Within the heavens shine:—
Give us, O Lord, fresh hopes in heaven,
　And trust in things divine.
4 Let peace, O Lord! thy peace, O God!
　Upon our souls descend,
From midnight fears, and perils, thou
　Our trembling hearts defend:
Give us a respite from our toil,
　Calm and subdue our woes;
Through the long day we suffer, Lord,
　O give us now repose!

　　　　　　　　　　Adelaide A. Procter.

SONGS OF WORSHIP.

TRURO. L. M.   CHARLES BURNEY.

1. Je-sus, thou ev-er-last-ing King, Ac-cept the trib-ute which we bring;
Ac-cept thy well-de-serv'd re-nown, And wear our prais-es as thy crown.

9

2 Let every act of worship be
Like our espousals, Lord, to thee;
Like the blest hour, when from above
We first received the pledge of love.

3 Let every moment as it flies,
Increase thy praise, improve our joys,
Till we are raised to sing thy Name,
At the great supper of the Lamb.
                               Isaac Watts.

MORNINGTON. S. M.   EARL OF MORNINGTON, AD. BY LOWELL MASON.

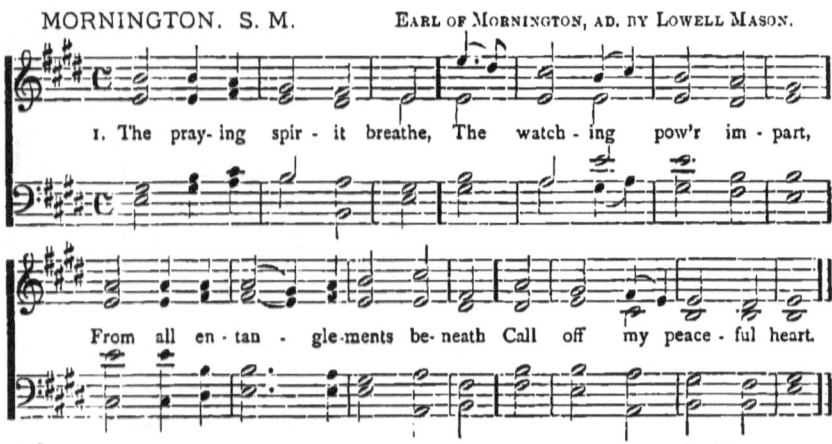

1. The pray-ing spir-it breathe, The watch-ing pow'r im-part,
From all en-tan-gle-ments be-neath Call off my peace-ful heart.

10   *The spirit of prayer.*

2 My feeble mind sustain,
By worldly thoughts oppressed;
Appear, and bid me turn again
To my eternal rest.

3 Swift to my rescue come,
Thine own this moment seize;

Gather my wandering spirit home,
And keep in perfect peace.

4 Suffered no more to rove
O'er all the earth abroad,
Arrest the prisoner of thy love,
And shut me up in God.
                     Charles Wesley.

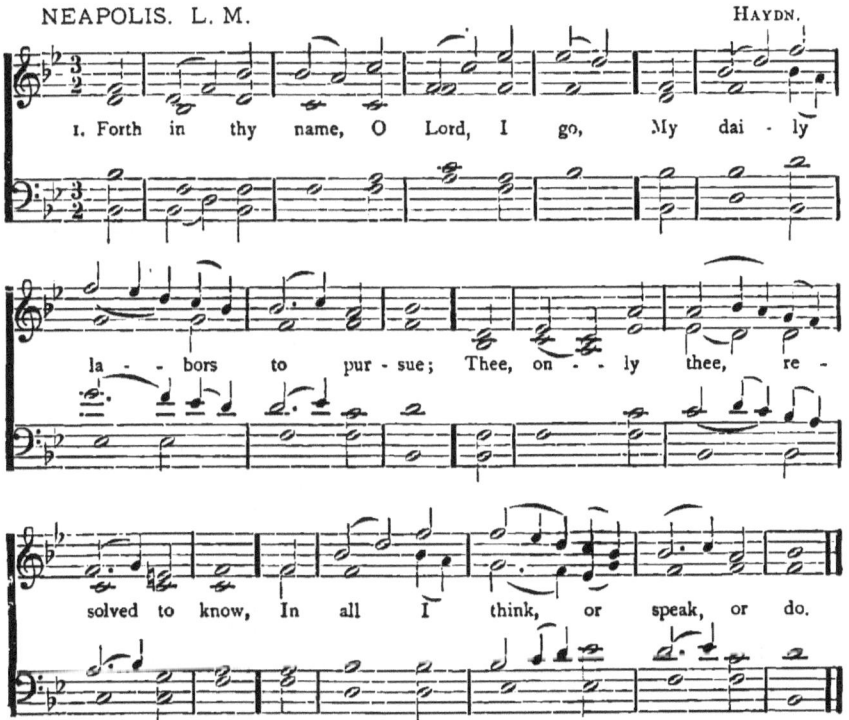

NEAPOLIS. L. M. — HAYDN.

1. Forth in thy name, O Lord, I go, My daily labors to pursue; Thee, only thee, resolved to know, In all I think, or speak, or do.

11 *"Walk before me, and be thou perfect."*

1 Forth in thy name, O Lord, I go,
   My daily labors to pursue;
Thee, only thee, resolved to know,
   In all I think, or speak, or do.

2 Thee will I set at my right hand,
   Whose eyes mine inmost substance see,
And labor on at thy command,
   And offer all my works to thee.

3 Give me to bear thy easy yoke,
   And every moment watch and pray;
And still to things eternal look,
   And hasten to thy glorious day.

4 For thee delightfully employ
   Whate'er thy bounteous grace hath given;
And run my course with even joy,
   And closely walk with thee to heaven.
                              Charles Wesley.

SONGS OF WORSHIP

PRAYER. — JOHN BEETHAM.

1. Pray, without ceasing pray, Your Captain gives the word; His summons cheerfully obey, And call upon the Lord.
To God your ev'ry want, In instant pray'r display; Pray always; pray and never faint, Pray, without ceasing pray.

CHORUS.
Ask, and it shall be given; Seek and ye shall find; Knock and the door shall be open'd unto you.

Copyright, 1891, by Hunt & Eaton.

12

2 In fellowship, alone
  To God with faith draw near;
Approach his courts, beseige his throne,
  With all the power of prayer.

His mercy now implore,
  And now show forth His praise;
In shouts, or silent awe adore
  His miracles of grace.

— Charles Wesley.

JESUS, SAVIOUR, PILOT ME. — J. E. GOULD.

Jesus, Saviour, pilot me, Over life's tempestuous sea;

SONGS OF WORSHIP.

JESUS, SAVIOUR, PILOT ME.—*Concluded.*

Un-known waves be-fore me roll, Hid-ing rock and treach'rous shoal;
Chart and com-pass come from thee: Je - sus, Sav - iour, pi - lot me.

13

2 As a mother stills her child,
Thou canst hush the ocean wild;
Boist'rous waves obey thy will,
When thou sayst to them "Be still!"
Wondrous Sover'ign of the sea,
Jesus, Saviour, pilot me.

3 When at last I near the shore,
And the fearful breakers roar
'Twixt me and the peaceful rest,
Then, while leaning on thy breast,
May I hear thee say to me,
"Fear not, I will pilot thee!"

Rev. Edward Hopper.

HEAR MY PRAYER. S. V. R. FORD.

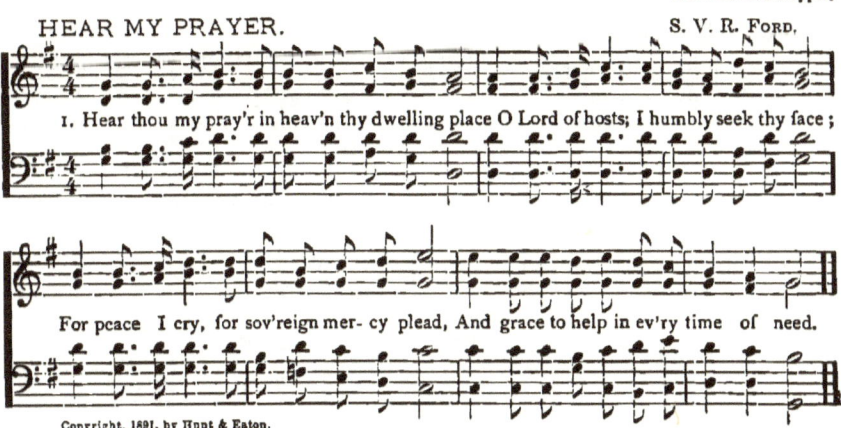

1. Hear thou my pray'r in heav'n thy dwelling place O Lord of hosts; I humbly seek thy face;
For peace I cry, for sov'reign mer-cy plead, And grace to help in ev'ry time of need.

Copyright, 1891, by Hunt & Eaton.

14

2 O hide thy face forever from my sin:
Cleanse me from guilt and make me pure within;
All pride destroy, all vanity remove
And make my heart the temple of thy love.

3 When dangers fierce beset my trembling soul
Be my defence, the tempters pow'r control;
When tempests rage my heart shall fear no ill,
If I but hear thee whisper, "Peace, be still!"

S. V. R. Ford.

PILGRIM, WATCH AND PRAY.
T. E. PERKINS.

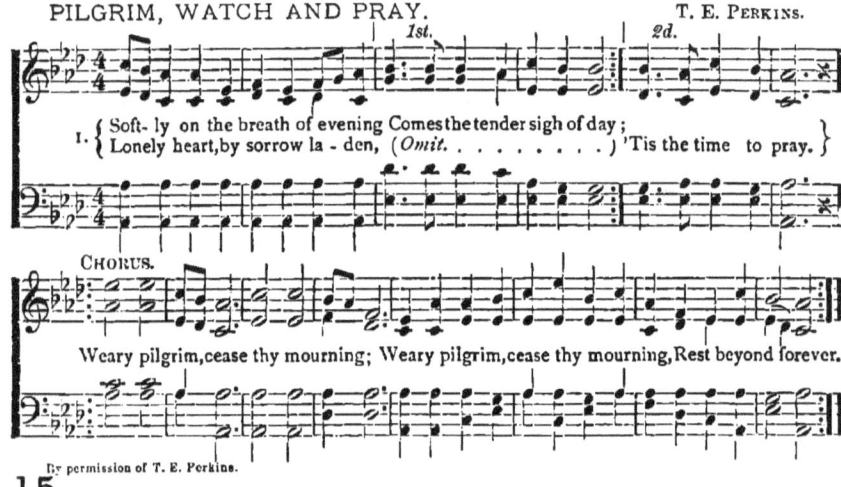

1. Soft-ly on the breath of evening Comes the tender sigh of day;
Lonely heart, by sorrow la-den, (*Omit*. . . . .) 'Tis the time to pray.

CHORUS.
Weary pilgrim, cease thy mourning; Weary pilgrim, cease thy mourning, Rest beyond forever.

By permission of T. E. Perkins.

15
2 'Tis the hour when hallowed feelings
Chase our doubts and fears away;
'Tis the hour for calm devotion,
Pilgrim, watch and pray.—CHO.

3 Though temptations dark oppress thee,
Jesus guides thee on thy way;
He will hear thy lightest whisper,
Pilgrim, watch and pray.—CHO.
Fanny Crosby.

MAINZER. L. M.
JOSEPH MAINZER.

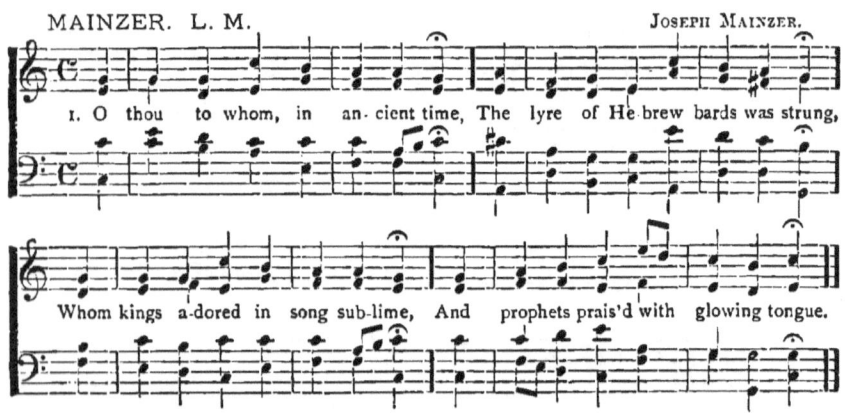

1. O thou to whom, in an-cient time, The lyre of Hebrew bards was strung,
Whom kings a-dored in song sub-lime, And prophets prais'd with glowing tongue.

16 *True worship every-where accepted.*

2 Not now on Zion's height alone
The favored worshiper may dwell,
Nor where, at sultry noon, thy Son
Sat weary by the patriarch's well.

3 From every place below the skies,
The grateful song, the fervent prayer,

The incense of the heart, may rise
To heaven, and find acceptance there.

4 O thou to whom, in ancient time,
The holy prophet's harp was strung,
To thee at last in every clime,
Shall temples rise and praise be sung.
John Pierpont.

SONGS OF WORSHIP.

IN THE ROSY LIGHT OF MORNING BRIGHT.

C. M. Wyman.

Used by permission of Oliver Ditson & Co.

17

2 Let his praise be spread, for the Lamb who bled
To deliver us from woe,
Has endured the cross, the disgrace, the loss,
Let his praise forever flow.—Cho.

3 Now exalted high over earth and sky,
He delights in mercy still;
Bends his gracious ear our requests to hear,
And our longing souls to fill.—Cho.

4 On the cross he hung for the old and young,
But he loves the children best;
To his arms we'll fly, on his grace rely,
And secure the promised rest.—Cho.

SONGS OF WORSHIP.

PRAISE THE LORD! YE HEAVENS, ADORE HIM.

Copyright, 1896, by W. J. Kirkpatrick.

18

2 Praise the Lord, for he hath spoken;
   Worlds his mighty voice obeyed;
Laws which never shall be broken
   For their guidance he hath made.—Cho.

3 Praise the Lord, for he is glorious;
   Never shall his promise fail;

God has made his saints victorious;
   Sin and death shall not prevail.—Cho.

4 Praise the God of our salvation;
   Hosts on high his power proclaim;
Heaven and earth, and all creation,
   Laud and magnify his name.—Cho.

John Kempthorne.

SONGS OF WORSHIP.

HEAVENLY FATHER, SEND THY BLESSING.

HENRY SMART.

1. Heavenly Father, send thy blessing On thy children gather'd here;
May they all, thy name confessing Be to thee forever dear.
Holy Saviour, who in meekness Didst vouchsafe a Child to be,
Guide their steps and help their weakness, Bless and make them like to thee. A-men.

19

2 Bear thy lambs when they are weary
In thine arms, and at thy breast;
Through life's desert, dry and dreary,
Bring them to thy heavenly rest.

Spread thy golden pinions o'er them,
Holy Spirit from above;
Guide them, lead them, go before them,
Give them peace, and joy, and love.

Bp. Christopher Wordsworth, D.D.

SWEET SAVIOUR, BLESS US ERE WE GO.

W. H. Monk.

Sweet Saviour, bless us ere we go: Thy words into our minds instill;
And make our luke-warm hearts to glow With lowly love and fervent will.
Through life's long day, and death's dark night, O gentle Jesu, be our light.

20

2 The day is gone, its hours have run,
And thou hast taken count of all,
The scanty triumphs grace hath won,
The broken vow, the frequent fall.
Thro' life's long day and death's dark night,
O gentle Jesu, be our light.

3 Grant us, dear Lord, from evil ways
True absolution and release;
And bless us, more than in past days,
With purity and inward peace.
Thro' life's long day and death's dark night,
O gentle Jesu, be our light.

4 Labor is sweet, for thou hast toiled;
And care is light, for thou hast cared;
Ah, never let our works be soiled
With strife, or by deceit ensnared.
Thro' life's long day and death's dark night,
O gentle Jesu, be our light.

5 For all we love, the poor, the sad,
The sinful, unto thee we call;
O let thy mercy make us glad;
Thou art our Jesus, and our all.
Thro' life's long day and death's dark night,
O gentle Jesu, be our light.

6 Sweet Saviour, bless us, night is come,
Through night and darkness near us be,
Good angels watch about our home,
And we are one day nearer thee.
Thro' life's long day and death's dark night,
O gentle Jesu, be our light.

F. W. Faber.

SONGS OF THE SABBATH.

SOFTLY FADES THE TWILIGHT RAY. H. S. C.

By permission.

21 *Sabbath evening.*

1 Softly fades the twilight ray
Of the holy Sabbath day;
Gently as life's setting sun,
When the Christian's course is run.

2 Night her solemn mantle spreads
O'er the earth as daylight fades;
All things tell of calm repose,
At the holy Sabbath's close.

3 Still the Spirit lingers near,
Where the evening worshiper
Seeks communion with the skies,
Pressing onward to the prize.

4 Saviour, may our Sabbaths be
Days of joy and peace in thee,
Till in heaven our souls repose,
Where the Sabbath ne'er shall close.
                              Samuel F. Smith.

SONGS OF THE SABBATH.

LISCHER. H. M.   LOWELL MASON.

1. Welcome, de-light-ful morn, Thou day of sacred rest;
We hail thy kind return; Lord make these moments blest; From the low train of mortal toys, We soar to reach im-mor-tal joys, We soar to reach im-mor-tal joys.

22 *Welcome, delightful morn.*

2 Now may the Lord descend
   And fill his throne of grace,
Thy sceptre, Lord, extend,
   While saints address thy face;
Let sinners feel thy quick'ning word,
And learn to know and fear the Lord.

3 Descend, celestial Dove!
   With all thy quick'ning powers;
Disclose a Saviour's love,
   And bless these sacred hours;
Then shall our souls new life obtain,
Nor Sabbath's be bestowed in vain.

FEDERAL STREET.   H. K. OLIVER.

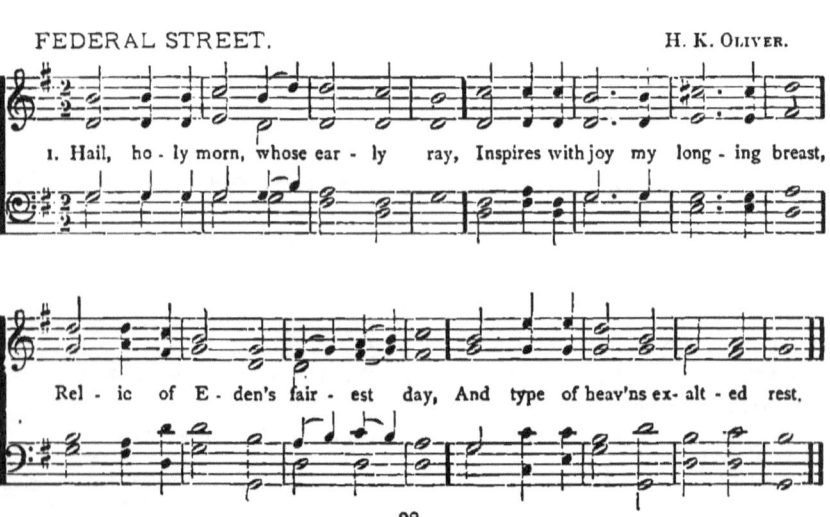

1. Hail, ho-ly morn, whose ear-ly ray, Inspires with joy my long-ing breast, Rel-ic of E-den's fair-est day, And type of heav'ns ex-alt-ed rest.

SONGS OF THE SABBATH.

FEDERAL STREET.—*Concluded.*

23 *Holy, holy morn.*

2 Thy sacred memories impart
  A charm to thy returning light;
  They thrill devotion's glowing heart,
  With rapt emotions of delight.

3 Hallow'd in Eden was the dawn
  That harbingered thy rising sun—
  Proclaiming night's dark veil withdrawn,
  The day of holy rest begun.

4 Sacred of old! thrice sacred now!
  On thee th'enshrouded Prince of Life
  Wrested the crown from Death's dark brow
  And rose triumphant from the strife.

5 Then hail! all hail! sweet Sabbath morn
  Let earth and heav'n their voices raise,
  To celebrate thy glad return,
  In anthems of divinest praise.
  S. V. R. Ford.

HUMMEL. C. M. H. C. ZEUNER.

1. The Lord of Sabbath let us praise; In concert with the blest,
   Who, joyful, in harmonious lays Employ an endless rest.

24 *Easter Sunday.*

1 The Lord of Sabbath let us praise,
  In concert with the blest,
  Who, joyful, in harmonious lays
  Employ an endless rest.

2 Thus, Lord, while we remember thee,
  We blest and pious grow;
  By hymns of praise we learn to be
  Triumphant here below.

3 On this glad day a brighter scene
  Of glory was displayed,
  By the eternal Word, than when
  This universe was made.

4 He rises, who mankind has bought
  With grief and pain extreme:
  'Twas great to speak the world from naught;
  'Twas greater to redeem.
  Samuel Wesley, Jr.

SONGS OF THE SABBATH.

COME, MY SOUL, THOU MUST BE WAKING.   J. Stainer.

25

1 Come, my soul, thou must be waking,
   Now is breaking
     O'er the earth another day:
   Come, to him who made this splendor
   See thou render
     All thy feeble strength can pay.

2 Gladly hail the sun returning:
   Ready burning
     Be the incense of thy powers:
   For the night is safely ended;
   God hath tended
     With his care thy helpless hours.

3 Pray that he may prosper ever
   Each endeavor,
     When thine aim is good and true;
   But that he may ever thwart thee,
   And convert thee,
     When thou evil wouldst pursue.

Rev. H. J. Buckoll.

SONGS OF THE SABBATH.

LORD! IN THE MORNING THOU SHALT HEAR.
S. Stanley.

26

1 Lord! in the morning thou shalt hear
   My voice ascending high;
   To thee will I direct my prayer,
   To thee lift up mine eye:—

2 Up to the hills, where Christ has gone
   To plead for all his saints,
   Presenting at his Father's throne,
   Our songs and our complaints.

3 Thou art a God, before whose sight,
   The wicked shall not stand;
   Sinners shall ne'er be thy delight,
   Nor dwell at thy right hand.

4 But to thy house will I resort,
   To taste thy mercies there;
   I will frequent thy holy court,
   And worship in thy fear.

5 Oh, may thy Spirit guide my feet,
   In ways of righteousness;
   Make every path of duty straight,
   And plain before my face.

Rev. Isaac Watts, D. D.

SONGS OF THE SABBATH.

CHIME ON.—*Concluded.*

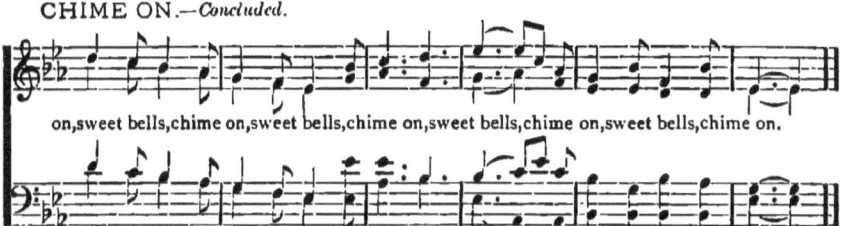

on, sweet bells, chime on, sweet bells, chime on, sweet bells, chime on, sweet bells, chime on.

27

2 We leave all cares this day,
To read the "Book Divine;"
There we are taught the way
To joys that ne'er decline;
The music sweet of Sabbath bells,
How gently on the ear it swells!
  Cho.—Chime on, &c.

3 We leave our earthly home,
To seek that blest abode,
Where loved companions come
To lift their hearts to God;
List to the sound, the sound that tells
The music of those Sabbath bells;
  Cho.—Chime on, &c.
      Australis.

SWEET IS THE WORK, O LORD.   J. BARNBY.

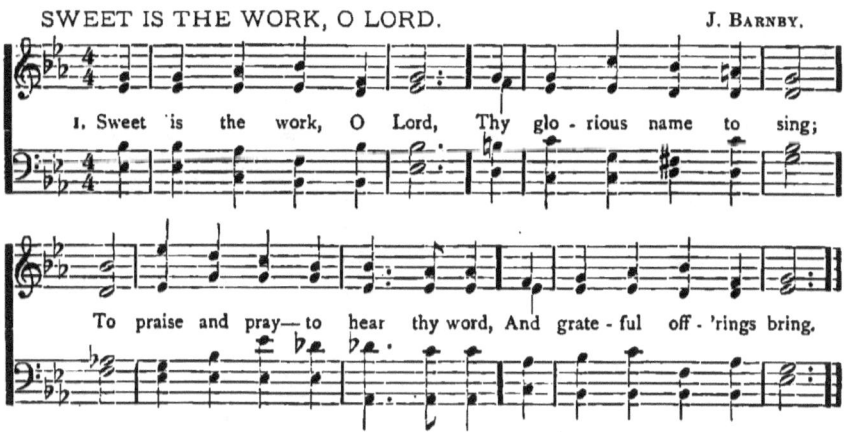

1. Sweet is the work, O Lord, Thy glo-rious name to sing;
To praise and pray—to hear thy word, And grate-ful off-'rings bring.

28

1 Sweet is the work, O Lord,
Thy glorious name to sing;
To praise and pray—to hear thy word,
And grateful offerings bring.

2 Sweet—at the dawning light,
Thy boundless love to tell;
And when approach the shades of night,
Still on the theme to dwell.

3 Sweet—on this day of rest,
To join in heart and voice,
With those who love and serve thee best,
And in thy name rejoice.

4 To songs of praise and joy
Be every Sabbath given,
That such may be our blest employ
Eternally in heaven.
        Miss Harriet Auber.

SONGS OF GOD.

OUR FATHER WATCHETH O'ER US.
S. V. R. Ford.

Copyright, 1891, by Hunt & Eaton.

29

2 Pities all our sorrows,
   Counteth all our tears;
Manifold his mercies,
   Better than our fears.—Ref.

3 Graciously he follows,
   If from him we stray;
Ever quick to hear us
   If to him we pray.—Ref.

4 Lovingly he calls us
   Back from paths of sin,
To the way of safety—
   Bids us walk therein.—Ref.

5 Faithfully he leads us,
   By his own right hand,
Through our pilgrim journey
   To the Fatherland.—Ref.

H. H. Green.

SONGS OF GOD.

30 *Holy, holy, holy Lord.*

2 Holy, holy, holy! thee,
  One Jehovah evermore,
 Father, Son, and Spirit! we,
  Dust and ashes, would adore;
 Lightly by the world esteemed,
 From that world by thee redeemed,
 Sing we here with glad accord,
 Holy, holy, holy Lord!

3 Holy, holy, holy! all
  Heaven's triumphant choir shall sing,
 While the ransomed nations fall
  At the footstool of their King:
 Then shall saints and seraphim,
 Harps and voices, swell one hymn,
 Blending in sublime accord,
 Holy, holy, holy Lord!
        James Montgomery.

SONGS OF GOD.

OLMUTZ. S. M.   Arr. by LOWELL MASON.

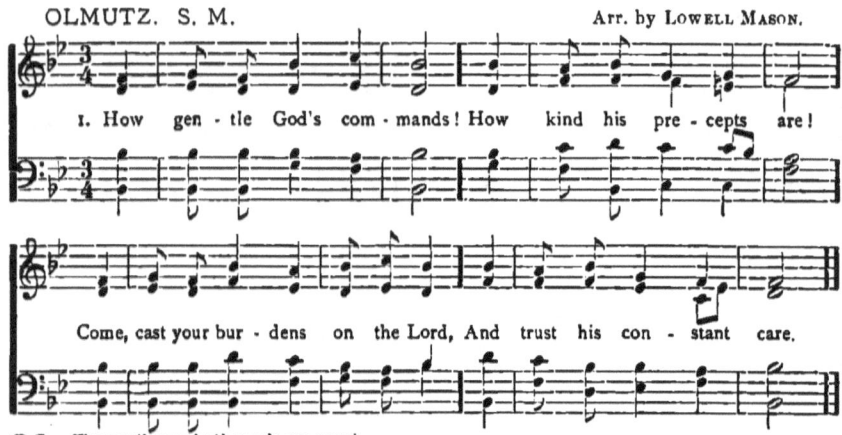

1. How gen-tle God's com-mands! How kind his pre-cepts are!
Come, cast your bur-dens on the Lord, And trust his con-stant care.

31 *Thy gentleness hath made me great.*
Ps. 18 : 35.

2 Beneath his watchful eye
His saints securely dwell;
That hand which bears all nature up
Shall guard his children well.

3 Why should this anxious load
Press down your weary mind?

Haste to your heavenly Father's throne,
And sweet refreshment find.

4 His goodness stands approved,
Unchanged from day to day:
I'll drop my burden at his feet,
And bear a song away.
                      Philip Doddridge.

SAWLEY. C. M.   PIGOU.

1. Shine on our souls, e-ter-nal God, With rays of beau-ty shine;
Oh, let thy fa-vor crown our days, And all their round be thine.

32 *Shine on our souls.*

2 With thee let every week begin,
With thee each day be spent,
For thee each fleeting hour employed,
Since each by thee is lent.

3 Thus cheer us through this desert road,
Till all our labors cease;
And heaven refresh our weary souls
With everlasting peace.
                      Philip Doddridge, 1740.

SONGS OF GOD.

A JOYFUL SONG. Mrs. Joseph F. Knapp.

1. Yes, I will bless thee, O my God, Thro' all my fleeting days; And to eternity prolong Thy vast, thy boundless praise.

CHORUS.
Thro' all eternity, to thee A joyful song I'll raise; But oh! eternity's too short To utter all thy praise, But oh! eternity's too short To utter all thy praise.

Copyright by Joseph F. Knapp.

33 *Perpetual praise.*

2 Nor shall my tongue alone proclaim
   The honours of my God;
My life, with all its active powers,
   Shall spread thy praise abroad.—Cho.

3 Nor will I cease thy praise to sing,
   When death shall close mine eyes;

My thoughts shall then to nobler heights
   And sweeter raptures rise.—Cho.

4 Then shall my lips, in endless praise,
   Their grateful tribute pay;
The theme demands an angel's tongue,
   And an eternal day.—Cho.

Heginbotham.

SONGS OF GOD.

BEMERTON. C. M.   Henry Wellington Greatorex.

34 *The Author of every perfect gift.*

2 Mercy and grace are thine alone,
  And power and wisdom too:
Without the Spirit of thy Son,
  We nothing good can do.

3 We cannot speak one useful word,
  One holy thought conceive,
Unless, in answer to our Lord,
  Thyself the blessing give.

4 His blood demands the purchased grace:
  His blood's availing plea
Obtained the help for all our race,
  And sends it down to me.

5 From thee, through Jesus, we receive
  The power on thee to call,
In whom we are, and move, and live;
  Our God is all in all.

Charles Wesley.

FORTRESS. 8, 7, 6.   Martin Luther.

SONGS OF GOD.

FORTRESS.—*Concluded.*

For still our an-cient foe Doth seek to work us woe; His craft and power are great,

And, arm - ed with cruel hate, On earth is not his e - - qual.

35 *God a mighty fortress.*

2 Did we in our own strength confide,
　Our striving would be losing;
　Were not the right man on our side,
　The man of God's own choosing.
Dost ask who that may be?
Christ Jesus, it is he;
Lord Sabaoth is his name,
From age to age the same,
　And he must win the battle.

3 That word above all earthly powers—
　No thanks to them—abideth;
　The Spirit and the gifts are ours
　Through him who with us sideth.
Let goods and kindred go,
This mortal life also:
The body they may kill:
God's truth abideth still,
　His kingdom is forever.

　　　Martin Luther. Tr. by F. H. Hedge.

GIVE YE TO JEHOVAH.　　　　　　H. R. PALMER.

1. Give ye to Je-ho-vah, O sons of the mighty, Give ye to Je ho- vah the glory and power:

Give ye to Je-ho-vah the hon- or and glo-ry; In beau-ty of ho - li-ness kneel and adore.

Copyright, 1878, by H. R. Palmer.

36
2 The voice of Jehovah comes down on the waters; [nigh:
　In thunder the God of the glory draws

Lo, over the waves of the wide-flowing waters
Jehovah as King is enthroned on high!

SONGS OF GOD.

37 *On our way rejoicing.*

2 If with honest-hearted love for God and man,
Day by day thou find us doing what we can,
Thou who giv'st the seed-time wilt give large increase, [with peace.—Cho.
Crown the head with blessings, fill the heart
3 On our way rejoicing gladly let us go;
Conquered hath our Leader, vanquished is our foe!
Christ without, our safety, Christ within our joy; [destroy?—Cho.
Who, if we be faithful, can our hope
4 Unto God the Father joyful songs we sing; [bring;
Unto God the Saviour thankful hearts we
Unto God the Spirit bow we and adore,
On our way rejoicing now and evermore.—Cho.

SONGS OF GOD.

38

2 No failure in his promises,
　But steadfast, firm and sure;
The word of our unchanging God
　Forever shall endure.
Though heaven and earth shall pass away,
　And all we love may die,
God's promises to us remain,—
　On these we may rely.—Cho.

3 Believing them, the Spirit's pow'r
　Renews and purifies,
Thro' Christ's all-cleansing, precious blood,
　Our perfect sacrifice.
O, glorious legacy of heaven,
　So rich, so vast and free,
These precious promises divine,
　Securing all to me.—Cho.

Mary D. James.

SONGS OF GOD.

STILL, STILL WITH THEE. Arr. Felix Mendelssohn Bartholdy, (1809-1847.)

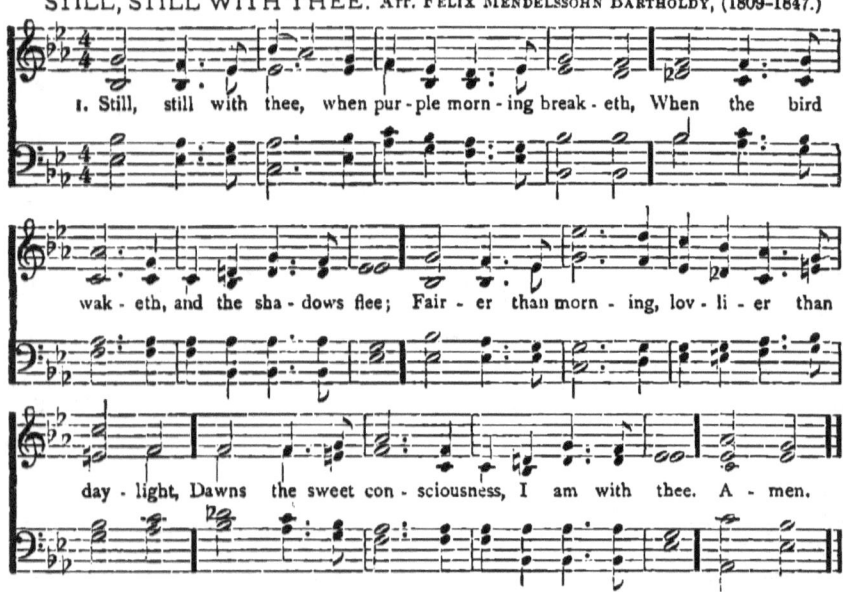

1. Still, still with thee, when purple morning breaketh, When the bird waketh, and the shadows flee; Fairer than morning, lovlier than daylight, Dawns the sweet consciousness, I am with thee. Amen.

39

2 Alone with thee, amid the mystic shadows,
 The solemn hush of nature newly born;
Alone with thee in breathless adoration,
 In the calm dew and freshness of the morn.

3 As in the dawning, o'er the waveless ocean,
 The image of the morning-star doth rest;
So in this stillness, thou beholdest only,
 Thine image in the waters of my breast.

4 Still, still to thee! as to each new-born morning,
 A fresh and solemn splendor still is given,
So does this blessed consciousness awaking,
 Breathe each day nearness unto thee and heaven.

5 When sinks the soul, subdued by toil, to slumber,
 Its closing eye looks up to thee in prayer;
Sweet the repose beneath thy wings o'ershading,
 But sweeter still, to wake and find thee there.

6 So shall it be at last, in that bright morning,
 When the soul waketh, and life's shadows flee;
O in that hour, fairer than daylight dawning,
 Shall rise the glorious thought—I am with thee. Amen.

Harriet Beecher Stowe (1814—), 1855.

PRAISE, MY SOUL, THE KING OF HEAVEN. 8s.7s. Six lines. German.

Bold.

1. Praise, my soul, the King of heaven, To his feet thy tribute bring;

SONGS OF GOD.

PRAISE, MY SOUL, ETC.—*Concluded.*

40

2 Praise him for his grace and favor,
　To our fathers in distress;
Praise him still the same as ever,
　Slow to chide, and swift to bless;
Alleluia! Alleluia!
　Glorious in his faithfulness.

3 Father-like, he tends and spares us,
　Well our feeble frame he knows;
In his hands he gently bears us,
　Rescues us from all our foes;
Alleluia! Alleluia!
　Widely yet his mercy flows

4 Angels in the height adore him!
　Ye behold him face to face;
Saints triumphant bow before him!
　Gathered in from every race:
Alleluia! Alleluia!
　Praise with us the God of grace.

DIJON. 7.   J. G. BITTHAUER.

41

2 Sovereign Father, heavenly King,
Thee we now presume to sing;
Thee with thankful hearts we prove
God of power, and God of love.

3 Christ our Lord and God we own,
Christ, the Father's only Son,
Lamb of God for sinners slain,
Saviour of offending man.

              Charles Wesley.

SONGS OF GOD.

HARK, HARK, MY SOUL! THY FATHER'S VOICE IS CALLING.

H. Smart.

1. Hark, hark, my soul! Thy Father's voice is call-ing,—E'en now it breathes o'er life's dark trou-bled sea; That gra-cious voice like heavenly dew is fall-ing; Hark, hark, my soul! the Fa-ther calls for thee. Fa-ther of mer-cy, Fa-ther of love! Thee would we fol-low to our own dear home a-bove!

Used by permission of Oliver Ditson & Co., owners of copyright.

42

2 Hark, hark, my soul! from heaven that voice is pleading
   With thee ere evil days draw darkly near;
   Now, in thy dawn, the Father's hand is leading,
   From sin and shame, from sorrow, doubt and fear.
   Father of mercy, Father of love!
   Thee would we follow to our own dear home above!

3 Hark, hark, my soul! still, still that voice is sounding,
   Like music sweet from some far distant shore;
   While angel bands, our daily path surrounding,
   Lead God's dear children on forever more.
   Father of mercy, Father of love!
   Thee would we follow to our own dear home above!

Rev. J. Page Hopps.

SONGS OF GOD.

GOD CARETH FOR ME.
C. E. ROWLEY.

1. O join with the worshiping angels to sing
Of God, our Creator, Preserver and King;
Transcendent in glory, in station most high,
He dazzles with splendor the sun in the sky.

Copyright, 1888, by C. E. Rowley.

43

2 All Nature proclaims him; the outermost Star
That hurries away on its mission afar,
Chants abroad, as it flies o'er the wondering earth,
The praises of God in the song of its birth.

3 The Sea shouts aloud to the cloud-cleaving hills,
The Vales swell the song with the music of [rills,

The earth is his footstool, and heaven his throne;
God reigneth forever, he reigneth alone.

4 His breath is the wind, and his robe is the light,
His voice is the thunder, his shadow is night;
He rides on the tempest, he walks on the sea,
Yet feedeth the sparrows, and careth for me

Rev. T. C. Reade

SONGS OF CHRIST.

JESUS LIVES. 7s, 8s.   S. Albinus.
Bold.

1. Jesus lives! no longer now Can thy terrors, Death, appall us; Jesus lives! by this we know Thou, O Grave, canst not enthrall us. Alleluia!

44

2 Jesus lives! henceforth is death
But the gate of life immortal;
This shall calm our trembling breath,
When we pass the gloomy portal.
    Alleluia!

3 Jesus lives! for us he died;
Then, alone to Jesus living,

Pure in heart may we abide,
Glory to our Saviour giving.
    Alleluia!

4 Jesus lives! our hearts know well
Nought from us his love shall sever;
Life, nor death, nor powers of hell
Tear us from his keeping ever.
    Alleluia!

HEART OF JESUS.   Wm. F. Sherwin.
With deep pathos.

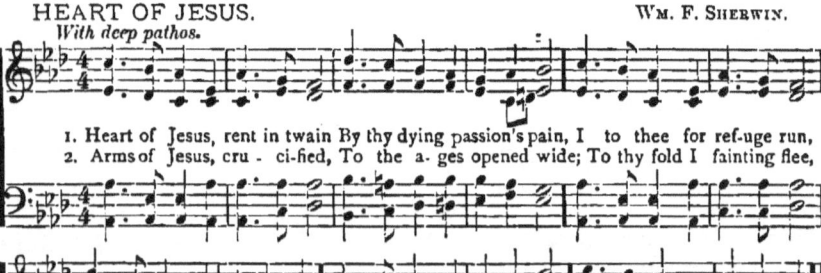

1. Heart of Jesus, rent in twain By thy dying passion's pain, I to thee for refuge run, Lifeless, loveless, and undone. From myself, and from my sin, Heart of Jesus, take me in!
2. Arms of Jesus, crucified, To the ages opened wide; To thy fold I fainting flee, From the foes that compass me. From myself, and from my sin, Arms of Jesus, take me in!

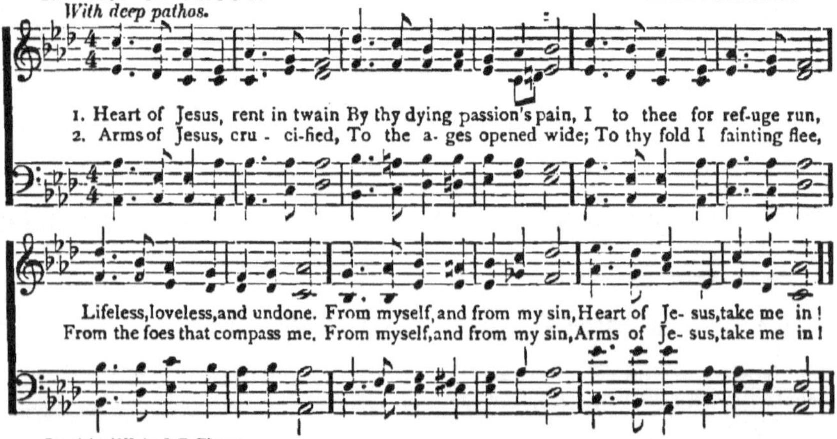

Copyright, 1888, by J. H. Vincent.

45

3 Love of Jesus, wider far
Than the widest heavens are;
Deeper than my sin can be,

Who shall separate from thee?
Safe from self and safe from sin,
Love of Jesus shut me in.

    Mary A. Lathbury.

SONGS OF CHRIST.

ALL ARE MINE. W. J. KIRKPATRICK, by per.

1. All the promises of Jesus, All his blessed words divine;
All his promises of favor, All are mine, forever mine.

REFRAIN.
All are mine, Oh, matchless mercy! Oh, how boundless is the store!
All his promises of favor, All are mine forever more.

Copyright, 1880, by W. J. Kirkpatrick.

2 All his promises of pardon,
  Coming from the throne above,
All his promises of cleansing,
  All his promises of love.—REF.

3 All his promises of comfort,
  Ev'ry promise of relief;

All his promises of gladness,
  Promises of joy in grief.—REF.

4 All his promises eternal,
  Honored in the ages past,
Words which must remain unbroken,
  Promises of heav'n at last.—REF.

Rev. E. H. Stokes, D.D.

SONGS OF CHRIST.

SING WITH ALL THE SONS OF GLORY.

Arr. fr. BEETHOVEN.

1. Sing with all the sons of glo-ry, Sing the res-ur-rec-tion song! Death and sor-row, earth's dark sto-ry, To the for-mer days be-long; All a-round the clouds are break-ing, Soon the storms of time shall cease, In God's like-ness, man a-wak-ing, Knows the ev-er-last-ing peace.

47

2 Oh, what glory, far exceeding
  All that eye has yet perceived!
Holiest hearts for ages pleading,
  Never that full joy conceived.
God has promised, Christ prepares it,
  There on high our welcome waits;
Every humble spirit shares it,
  Christ has passed th'eternal gates.

3 Life eternal! heaven rejoices,
  Jesus lives who once was dead;
Join, O man, the deathless voices,
  Child of God, lift up thy head!
Patriarchs from the distant ages,
  Saints all longing for their heaven,
Prophets, psalmists, seers and sages,
  All await the glory given.

4 Life eternal! oh, what wonders
  Crowd on faith; what joy unknown,
When, amidst earth's closing thunders,
  Saints shall stand before the throne!
Oh, to enter that bright portal,
  See that glowing firmament,
Know, with thee, O God immortal,
  " Jesus Christ whom thou hast sent!"

Rev. William J. Irons, D.D.

SONGS OF CHRIST.

THE FIRST NOWELL. * OLD STYLE.

48

2 They looked up and saw a star,
Shining in the east, beyond them far,
And to the earth it gave great light,
And so it continued both day and night.

3 And by the light of that same star,
Three wise men came from country far;
To seek for a King was their intent,
And to follow the star wherever it went.

4 This star drew nigh to the north-west,
O'er Bethlehem it took its rest,
And there it did both stop and stay,
Right over the place where Jesus lay.

5 There entered in those wise men three,
Full reverently upon their knee,
And offered there in his presence,
Their gold, and myrrh, and frankincense.

6 Then let us all with one accord,
Sing praises to our heavenly Lord,
That hath made heaven and earth of nought,
And with his blood mankind hath bought.

* The word Noël, or Nowell, or Nowel, signifies Christmas, but is more specifically applied to a Christmas Carol. It is from the French word *Nouvelles*, "tidings."

SONGS OF CHRIST.

WORGAN. *Joyful.*   HENRY CAREY.

1. Christ, the Lord is risen to-day, Hal - le - lu - jah!
Sons of men and an-gels say; Hal - le - lu - jah!
Raise your joys and tri - umphs high; Hal - le - lu - jah!
Sing, ye heav'ns, and earth re - ply. Hal - le - lu - jah!

49   *Christ is risen.*

2 Love's redeeming work is done; Hallelujah!
Fought the fight, the battle won: Hallelujah!
Lo! the sun's eclipse is o'er; Hallelujah!
Lo! he sets in blood no more. Hallelujah!

3 Vain the stone, the watch, the seal, Hallelujah!
Christ has burst the gates of hell: Hallelujah!
Death in vain forbids his rise; Hallelujah!
Christ hath opened paradise. Hallelujah!

4 Lives again our glorious King; Hallelujah!
Where, O Death, is now thy sting? Hallelujah!
Once he died our souls to save; Hallelujah!
Where's thy victory, boasting Grave? Hallelujah!

Charles Wesley.

SONGS OF CHRIST.

WELCOME, HAPPY MORNING. 5s.
A. S. Sullivan.

50

2 Earth with joy confesses, clothing her for Spring,
All good gifts returned with her returning King:
Bloom in every meadow, leaves on every bough,
Speak his sorrows ended, hail his triumph now.
Hell to-day is vanquished; Heaven is won to-day.

3 Maker and Redeemer, Life and Health to all,
Thou from Heaven beholding human nature's fall,
Of the Father's Godhead true and only Son,
Manhood to deliver, manhood didst put on.
Hell to-day is vanquished; Heaven is won to-day!

4 Thou, of Life the Author, death didst undergo,
Tread the path of darkness, saving strength to show;
Come, then, True and Faithful, now fulfil thy word,
'Tis thine own Third Morning! Rise, O buried Lord!
"Welcome, happy morning!" age to age shall say.

5 Loose the souls long prisoned, bound with Satan's chain;
All that now is fallen raise to life again;
Show thy face in brightness, bid the nations see;
Bring again our day-light; day returns with thee!
Hell to-day is vanquished; Heaven is won to-day.

SONGS OF CHRIST.

THE NAME OF JESUS.
S. V. R. Ford.

1. I love the name of Je-sus, I love but can-not tell The sweetness of his

presence, As he in me doth dwell. And thro' the bright for-ev-er, My

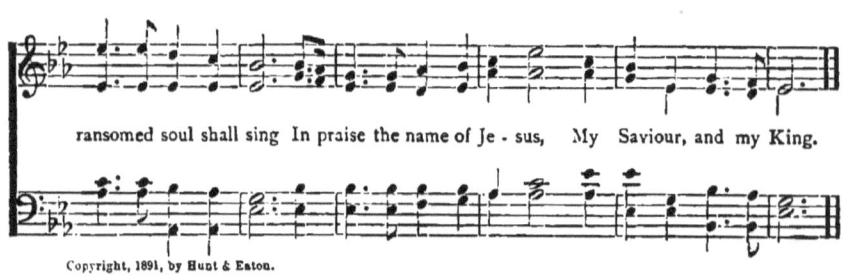

ransomed soul shall sing In praise the name of Je-sus, My Saviour, and my King.

Copyright, 1891, by Hunt & Eaton.

51

2 I love the name of Jesus,
   I love it more and more,
   Because the pain and sorrow
   Of sin for me he bore—Ref.

3 I love the name of Jesus,
   It grows to me more dear
   As through life's joys and trials
   I find him ever near.—Ref.

4 I love the name of Jesus,
   My dearest, truest Friend,
   Whose loving hand will guide me,
   Unto my journey's end.—Ref.

5 I love the name of Jesus,
   Eternally the same,
   I love, I love the Saviour,
   I love his precious name.—Ref.
                Rev. Frank E. Graeff.

SONGS OF CHRIST.

WHEN MARSHALED ON THE NIGHTLY PLAIN.

1. When, marshaled on the night-ly plain, The glittering host be-stud the sky, One star a-lone of all the train, Can fix the sin-ner's wand'ring eye. Hark! hark! to God the cho-rus breaks From ev-'ry host, from ev-'ry gem; But one a-lone the Sav-iour speaks, It is the Star of Beth-le-hem.

52 *"They saw the Star."*

2 Once on the raging seas I rode,
   The storm was loud, the night was dark,
The ocean yawned, and rudely blowed
   The wind that tossed my foundering bark.
Deep horror then my vitals froze;
   Death-struck, I ceased the tide to stem;
When suddenly a star arose,—
   It was the Star of Bethlehem!

3 It was my guide, my light, my all;
   It bade my dark forebodings cease,
And through the storm and danger's thrall
   It led me to the port of peace.
Now safely moored, my perils o'er,
   I'll sing, first in night's diadem,
For ever and for evermore,
   The Star, the Star of Bethlehem!

H. K. White.

SONGS OF CHRIST.

THE BANNER OF THE CROSS.
WALTER R. JOHNSTON.

1. Ye that love the name of Jesus, Lift his glorious banner high;
Float it out upon the breezes, Let it catch the sinner's eye.

CHORUS.
Hail the banner of the cross, O'er the world its folds shall wave,
All besides is worthless dross, This alone the world can save.

Copyright, 1891, by Hunt & Eaton.

53

2 Lift it high upon the mountain,
    Spread its folds in every vale,
Let it float beside the fountain,
    Till the world its beauties hail.—CHO.

3 Youthful hands aloft may bear it,
    Children rally 'neath its folds,

What an honor, all may share it,
    God from none his grace withholds.—CHO.

4 Glorious banner! rally round it,
    Bear it on triumphantly,
Sin's dark hosts shall ne'er confound it,
    It shall float eternally.—CHO.

W. Bennett.

SONGS OF CHRIST.

THE BETHLEHEM BABE.
H. R. Palmer.

1. Sweet, sweet, sweet the swell, The swell of Sabbath bell; But sweet-er still the notes of praise, The notes of praise our voic-es raise When Je-sus' love we're tell-ing, When Je-sus' love we're tell-ing A-men.

Copyright, 1887, by H. R. Palmer.

55

2 Cold! cold! cold the night,
The night was starry bright,
When Shepherds heard the angel note,
The angel note from heav'n afloat,
 That told to earth the story,
 That told to earth the story.

3 Low, low, low the bed,
The bed on which his head
Among the beasts was pillowed there—
Was pillowed there 'mid want and care,
 When God became incarnate,
 When God became incarnate.

4 Love, love, love unknown!
Unknown to leave a throne,
A fallen race from death to save,
From death to save, and in the grave
 To lay his head so Kingly,
 To lay his head so Kingly.

5 Loud, loud, loud we'll raise,
We'll raise our notes of praise!
The Bethlehem Babe in manger laid,
In manger laid, to death betrayed,
 We'll sing, we'll sing for ever,
 We'll sing, we'll sing for ever

JESUS, THESE EYES HAVE NEVER SEEN.
Geo. Kingsley.

1. Je-sus, these eyes have nev-er seen That ra-diant form of thine!

SONGS OF CHRIST.

JESUS, THESE EYES HAVE NEVER SEEN.—*Concluded.*

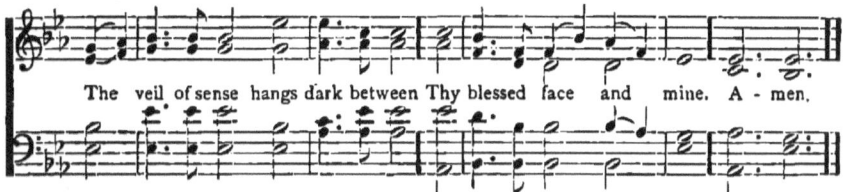

56

2 I see thee not, I hear thee not,
  Yet thou art oft with me;
  And earth hath ne'er so dear a spot,
  As where I meet with thee.
3 Like some bright dream that comes unsought,
  When slumbers o'er me roll,

Thine image ever fills my thought,
  And charms my ravished soul.

4 Yet though I have not seen, and still
  Must rest in faith alone;
  I love thee, dearest Lord!—and will,
  Unseen, but not unknown.
  Rev. Ray Palmer, tr.

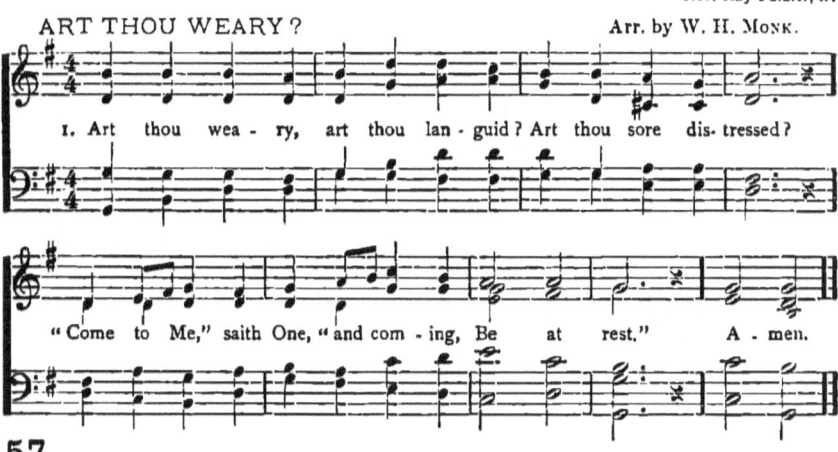

57

2 Hath he marks to lead me to him,
  If he be my guide?
  "In his feet and hands are wound-prints,
  And his side."
3 Is there diadem, as monarch,
  That his brow adorns?
  "Yes, a crown in very surety,
  But of thorns!"
4 If I find him, if I follow,
  What his guerdon here?
  "Many a sorrow, many a labor,
  Many a tear."

5 If I still hold closely to him,
  What hath he at last?
  "Sorrow vanquished, labor ended,
  Jordan past."
6 If I ask him to receive me,
  Will he say me nay?
  "Not till earth and not till heaven
  Pass away."
7 Finding, following, keeping, struggling,
  Is he sure to bless?
  "Saints, apostles, prophets, martyrs,
  Answer, Yes."
  Rev. John Mason Neale.

SONGS OF CHRIST.

PRINCETHORPE. 6s, 5s. D.
Moderato.

1. Je-sus is our Shep-herd, Well we know his voice; How the gentlest whis-per, Makes our hearts re-joice! E-ven when he chid-eth, Ten-der, is his tone; None but he shall guide us; We are his a-lone. A-men.

58 *Jesus our Shepherd.*

2 Jesus is our Shepherd;
   Guided by his arm,
Though the wolves may raven,
   None can do as harm;
When we tread death's valley,
   Dark with fearful gloom,
We will fear no evil,
   Victors o'er the tomb.

3 Jesus is our Shepherd;
   With his goodness now
And his tender mercy,
   He doth us endow!
Let us sing his praises
   With a gladsome heart,
Till in heaven we meet him,
   Never more to part.

INNOCENTS 7s.   ANON. Arr. by W. H. MONK.

1. At the Lamb's high feast we sing Praise to our vic-to-rious King,

SONGS OF CHRIST.

INNOCENTS.—*Concluded.*

Who hath washed us in the tide Flow-ing from his pierc-ed side.

59 *Praise to our victorious King.*

2 Praise we Christ, whose blood was shed,
Paschal Victim, paschal Bread;
With sincerity and love
Eat we manna from above.

3 Mighty Victim from the sky!
Hell's fierce powers beneath thee lie;

Thou hast conquered in the fight,
Thou hast brought us life and light:

4 Now no more can death appall,
Now no more the grave enthrall;
Thou hast opened paradise,
And in thee thy saints shall rise.

Roman Breviary. Tr. by R. Campbell.

JESUS, ONLY JESUS.   J. H. TENNEY, by per.

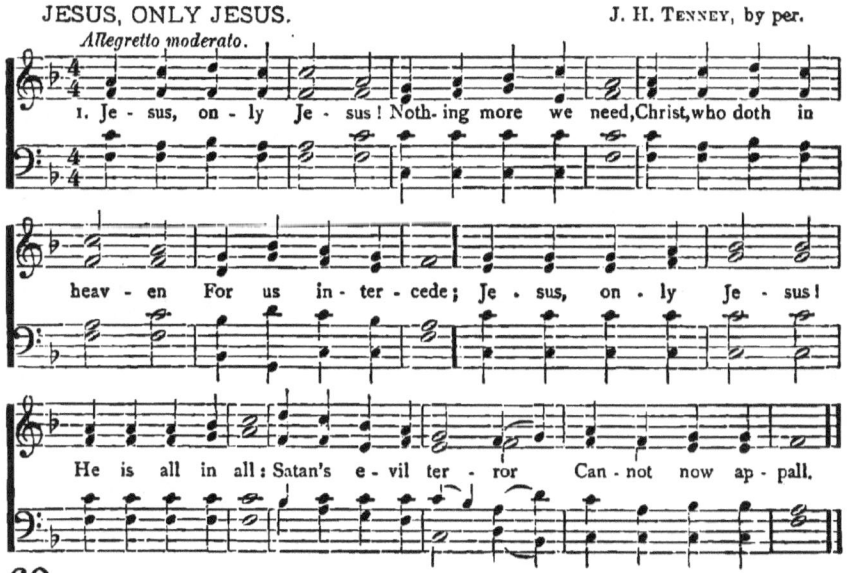

1. Je-sus, on-ly Je-sus! Noth-ing more we need, Christ, who doth in heav-en For us in-ter-cede; Je-sus, on-ly Je-sus! He is all in all: Satan's e-vil ter-ror Can-not now ap-pall.

60

2 Jesus, blessed Jesus!
  Came from heav'n above,
  Bore our pains and sorrows,
  Proving "God is love."
  More and more like Jesus
  May we ever grow:
  In our daily duties,
  Love to Jesus show.

3 Jesus, holy Jesus!
  Bids us God to serve;
  From that blest obedience
  May we never swerve!
  Jesus, faithful Jesus,
  Never will forsake;
  From his constant presence
  Let us courage take.

SONGS OF CHRIST.

WHO IS THIS?
H. P. Danks.

61

2 Who is this—a Man of Sorrows
  Walking sadly life's hard way,
Homeless, weary, sighing, weeping
  Over sin and Satan's sway?
'Tis our God, our glorious Saviour,
  Who above the starry sky
Now for us a place prepareth,
  Where no tear can dim the eye.

3 Who is this—behold him shedding
  Drops of blood upon the ground?
Who is this—despised, rejected,
  Mocked, insulted, beaten, bound?

'Tis our God, who gifts and graces
  On his Church now poureth down,
Who shall smite in holy vengeance
  All his foes beneath his throne.

4 Who is this that hangeth dying,
  While the rude world scoffs and scorns,
Numbered with the malefactors,
  Torn with nails, and crown'd with thorns?
'Tis the God, who ever liveth
  'Mid the shining ones on high,
In the glorious golden city
  Reigning everlastingly!

SONGS OF CHRIST.

'TIS SO SWEET TO TRUST IN JESUS. W. J. Kirkpatrick, by per.

Copyright, 1882, by W. J. Kirkpatrick.

62

2 O, how sweet to trust in Jesus,
  Just to trust his cleansing blood;
Just in simple faith to plunge me
  'Neath the healing, cleansing flood.—Ref.

3 Yes, 'tis sweet to trust in Jesus,
  Just from sin and self to cease;

Just from Jesus simply taking
  Life, and rest, and joy, and peace.—Ref.

4 I'm so glad I learned to trust thee,
  Precious Jesus, Saviour, Friend;
And I know that thou art with me,
  Wilt be with me to the end.—Ref.

Mrs. Louisa M. R. Stead.

SONGS OF CHRIST.

SILENT NIGHT.
MICHAEL HAYDN.

1. Si - lent night! Ho - ly night! All is calm, All is bright
Round yon vir - gin moth - er and Child! Ho - ly In - fant, so ten - der and mild,
Sleep in heav - en - ly peace, Sleep in heav - en - ly peace.

63

2 Silent night! Holy night!
Shepherds quake at the sight!
Glories stream from Heaven afar
Heavenly hosts sing Alleluia.
Christ, the Saviour, is born!
Christ, the Saviour, is born!

3 Silent night! Holy night!
Son of God, love's pure light
Radiant beams from thy holy face,
With the dawn of redeeming grace,
Jesus, Lord, at thy birth,
Jesus, Lord, at thy birth.

TRUSTING IN JESUS.
WALTER R. JOHNSTON.

1. Thou Son of God, my in - most soul With all its wants to thee is known;

SONGS OF CHRIST.

TRUSTING IN JESUS.—*Concluded.*

Thou on-ly canst its ways con-trol: Thy power can save, and thine a-lone.

64 Copyright, 1891, by Hunt & Eaton.

2 Thou know'st my longing heart aspires
Thy love to know, thine all to be!
But, Lord, these are but vain desires
Unless thy Spirit leadeth me.

3 May I the simple lesson learn
To trust thy word, in thee t'abide;
And as from earthly hope I turn
Be thou my strength, be thou my guide.

4 O Spirit of the living God,
Wilt thou now take me as thine own;
Make me, who paths of sin have trod,
An heir to an eternal throne?

5 O glorious truth! thou dost receive!
The cleansing of thy blood I feel!
I do in Jesus' power believe,
On me is set the Spirit's seal.

By Rev. C. C. Wilbor, Ph. D.

HAIL, TO THE LORD'S ANOINTED.   FROM LINDEMAN'S KORAL BOK.

1. { Hail, to the Lord's A-noin-ted, Great David's greater Son!
    Hail, in the time ap-point-ed, His reign on earth be-gun! } He comes to break oppression,
To set the cap-tive free; To take a-way trans-gres-sion, And rule in eq-ui-ty.

65 *The glories of Christ's kingdom.*

2 He comes with succor speedy
To those who suffer wrong;
To help the poor and needy,
And bid the weak be strong;
To give them songs for sighing,
Their darkness turn to light,
Whose souls, condemned and dying,
Were precious in his sight.

3 He shall descend like showers
Upon the fruitful earth,
And love and joy, like flowers,
Spring in his path to birth:

Before him, on the mountains,
Shall peace, the herald, go,
And righteousness, in fountains,
From hill to valley flow.

4 To him shall prayer unceasing,
And daily vows ascend;
His kingdom still increasing,
A kingdom without end:
The tide of time shall never
His covenant remove;
His name shall stand forever;
That name to us is Love.

James Montgomery.

SONGS OF CHRIST.

PRINCE OF PEACE.   Robert L. Fletcher.

1. Prince of peace, the Lord's Anoint-ed, Whom the prophets did fore-tell; In the time that God ap-point-ed, Lo, he comes on earth to dwell; Mild he leaves his home in glo-ry For the man-ger in the stall; Roy-al Babe of sa-cred sto-ry! An-gels hail him Lord of all, An-gels hail him Lord of all.

Copyright, 1890, by Robert L. Fletcher.

66

2 Prince of peace, and King forever,
   He shall rule the world alone;
Through all ages he will never
   Leave again his lofty throne;
Peacefully his reign is spreading
   To the confines of the earth;
Grace and truth his Spirit shedding
   O'er the world that gave him birth.

3 Prince of peace! his name how glorious!
   Victor-crowns adorn his brow;
O'er his mortal foes victorious;—
   Raise the voice of triumph now!
Shout, ye heralds of salvation,
   Give the tidings joyful wings!
Bear the news to every nation,
   Jesus reigns the King of kings.

                                              R. L. F.

SONGS OF CHRIST.

THE JOYFUL MORN.

67

2 High strains of praise are swelling
   From angel hosts on high,
And one soft voice is telling
   Glad tidings from the sky;
Tidings of free salvation,
   Of peace on earth below;
Through every land and nation
   The blessed word shall go!

3 His children's songs shall name him
   In many a tongue to-day;
His Church shall yet proclaim him
   To people far away;
Till idols fall before him,
   Till strife and wrong shall cease,
Till all the earth adore him,
   The eternal Prince of Peace!

SONGS OF CHRIST.

THE DAY OF RESURRECTION. H. SMART.

1. The day of res-ur-rec-tion, Earth, tell it out a-broad: The Pass-o-ver of glad-ness, The Pass-o-ver of God. From death to life e-ter-nal, From earth un-to the sky, Our Christ hath brought us o-ver, With hymns of vic-to-ry.

68

2 Our hearts be pure from evil,
　That we may see aright
The Lord in rays eternal
　Of resurrection light;
And, list'ning to his accents,
　May hear, so calm and plain,
His own " All hail! " and, hearing,
　May raise the victor-strain.

3 Now let the heavens be joyful,
　And earth her song begin,
The round world keep high triumph,
　And all that is therein;
Let all things seen and unseen
　Their notes of gladness blend,
For Christ the Lord is risen,
　Our Joy that hath no end.

Rev. John M. Neale, tr.

SONGS OF CHRIST.

GLORY TO GOD! PEACE ON EARTH!   EMMELAR.

69

2 Praise ye the Lord! lift to his name
  High hallelujahs from each happy voice;
Strike the loud chord! praise ye the Lord!
  Let every soul in his glory rejoice!
Oh, for a strain such as angels repeat,
    When the redeem'd cast their crowns at his feet;
  "Worthy the Lamb! once he was slain,
    Now on his throne he is reigning again!"

3 O Christ of God! risen and crowned!
  Come with thy presence, thy Spirit impart!
Come with thy love! come with thy power!
  Breathe on our souls, and enrich every heart!
Sad were thy sufferings, shameful thy cross,
  Sharing our punishment, bearing our loss;
Now, Lord of all, thee we adore!
  Bring we our souls to be thine evermore!

                            Rev. Charles S. Robinson, D.D.

SONGS OF CHRIST.

COME, JESUS, REDEEMER.
T. E. Perkins, by per.

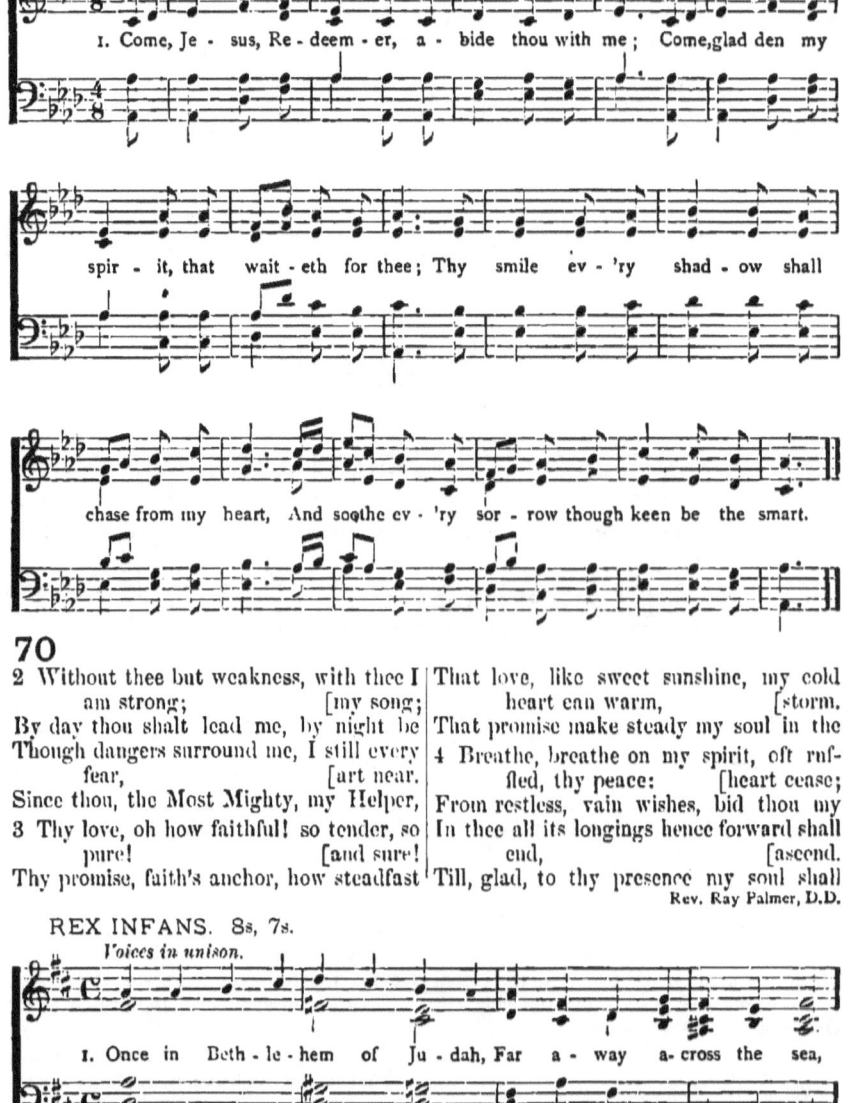

1. Come, Jesus, Redeemer, abide thou with me; Come, gladden my spirit, that waiteth for thee; Thy smile ev'ry shadow shall chase from my heart, And soothe ev'ry sorrow though keen be the smart.

70

2 Without thee but weakness, with thee I am strong; [my song;
By day thou shalt lead me, by night be
Though dangers surround me, I still every fear, [art near.
Since thou, the Most Mighty, my Helper,

3 Thy love, oh how faithful! so tender, so pure! [and sure!
Thy promise, faith's anchor, how steadfast

That love, like sweet sunshine, my cold heart can warm, [storm.
That promise make steady my soul in the

4 Breathe, breathe on my spirit, oft ruffled, thy peace: [heart cease;
From restless, vain wishes, bid thou my
In thee all its longings henceforward shall end, [ascend.
Till, glad, to thy presence my soul shall

Rev. Ray Palmer, D.D.

REX INFANS. 8s, 7s.

Voices in unison.

1. Once in Bethlehem of Judah, Far away across the sea,

SONGS OF CHRIST.

REX INFANS.—*Concluded.*

There was laid a lit-tle Ba-by On a Vir-gin Moth-er's knee.

REFRAIN.

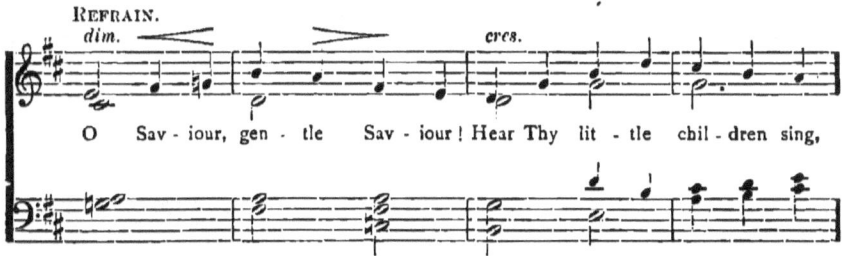

O Sav-iour, gen-tle Sav-iour! Hear Thy lit-tle chil-dren sing,

The God of our sal-va-tion, The Child that is our King.

71 *Once in Bethlehem.*

2 It was not a stately palace
   Where that little Baby lay,
With his servants to attend him,
   And with guards to keep the way.—Ref.

3 But the oxen stood around him
   In a stable, low and dim:
In the world he had created
   There was not a room for him.—Ref.

4 For he left his Father's glory,
   And the golden halls above,
And he took our human nature
   In the greatness of his love.—Ref.

5 Of his infinite compassion
   He can feel our want and woe;
For he suffered, he was tempted,
   When he lived our life below.—Ref.

6 Still his childhood's bright example
   Gives a light to our poor homes;
From the blood of his atoning
   Still our hope of pardon comes.—Ref.

7 Still he stands and pleads in heaven
   For us, weak and sin-defiled,—
God, who is a man for ever,
   Jesus, who was once a Child—Ref.

SONGS OF CHRIST.

THE ROSE OF SHARON.*
Words and Music by H. R. PALMER.

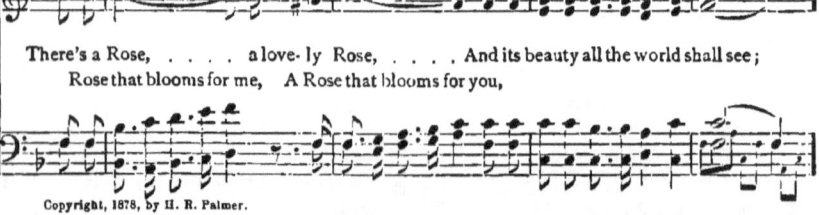

1. There's a Rose that is blooming for you, friend, There's a Rose that is blooming for me;

Its perfume is per-vad-ing the world, friend, Its perfume is for you and for me.

REFRAIN.

There's a Rose, ... a love-ly Rose, ... And its beauty all the world shall see;
Rose that blooms for me, A Rose that blooms for you,

Copyright, 1878, by H. R. Palmer.

* Of the many names given to our Saviour, "The Rose of Sharon" is the most beautiful. This little hymn was written on the shores of the Mediterranean, amid the fragrance of ever-blooming roses, and beneath the matchless beauty of Italian skies. Thoughts of the Holy Land on the farther shore, and of the purity and loveliness of the life of our Saviour mingled unconsciously with the surrounding beauty, and took form in this little poem and melody.

SONGS OF CHRIST.

THE ROSE OF SHARON.—*Concluded.*

There's a Rose, ... a love-ly Rose, ... Its perfume is for you and for me.
Rose that blooms for me, A Rose that blooms for you,

72
2 Long ago in the valley so fair, friend,
Far away by the beautiful sea,
This pure Rose in its beauty first bloom'd, friend,
And it blooms still for you and for me.

3 All in vain did they crush this fair flow'r, friend,
All in vain did they shatter the tree,
For its roots, deeply bedded, sprang forth, friend,
And it blooms still for you and for me.

HOW I LOVE JESUS. C. M.

AMERICAN SPIRITUAL.

1. There is a name I love to hear, I love to sing its worth; It sounds like music in mine ear—The sweetest name on earth.

CHORUS.

Oh, how I love Je-sus, Oh, how I love Je-sus, Oh, how I love Je-sus, Because he first loved me.

73 *The Dearest Name.*

2 It tells me of a Savior's love,
Who died to set me free;
It tells me of his precious blood,
The sinner's perfect plea.

3 It tells me what my Father hath
In store for every day,

And, though I tread a darksome path,
Yields sunshine all the way.

4 It tells of One, whose loving heart
Can feel my deepest woe,
Who in each sorrow bears a part,
That none can bear below.

Frederick Whitfield, 1859.

SONGS OF CHRIST.

HAIL SACRED MORN.—*Concluded.*

74

2 A radiance lights the Victor's brow,
  As he ascends on high;
He lives, our glorious Sov'reign now,
  He lives no more to die;
The portals in the sky swing wide,
  And harps of glory ring,
For death gives back the Prince who died,
  To be forever King.

3 We celebrate the day he rose,
  A victor from the grave;
Triumphant now o'er all his foes,
  He still delights to save;
He dwells in realms of bliss above,
  Who suffered here in pain;
And sends the blessing of his love
  Through all his righteous reign.
         R. L. F.

THE PRECIOUS LOVE OF JESUS. W. J. KIRKPATRICK, by per.

1. O sing the pow'r of love di-vine, The pre-cious love of Je-sus, That bids the light in dark-ness shine And wins the lost to Je-sus.

CHORUS.
O precious, pure, un-changing love, The bound-less love of Je-sus; It binds our hearts in un-ion sweet, And makes us one in Je-sus.

Copyright, 1885, by W. J. Kirkpatrick.

75

1 'Tis love that conquers every fear,
  The precious love of Jesus,
And now by faith has brought us near
  The bleeding side of Jesus.—CHO.

3 'Tis love that fills the joyful heart,
  And draws it up to Jesus,
Where neither life nor death can part
  The sacred bonds from Jesus.—CHO.

4 When faith and hope have ceas'd to shine,
  And we are safe with Jesus,
We'll praise the power of love divine
  That brought us home to Jesus —CHO.
         Fanny J. Crosby.

SONGS OF CHRIST.

THERE IS A GREEN HILL FAR AWAY.
R. S. WILLIS.

1. There is a green hill far away, Without a city wall,
Where the dear Lord was crucified, Who died to save us all.
We may not know, we cannot tell What pains he had to bear;
But we believe it was for us He hung and suffer'd there.

76

2 He died that we might be forgiven,
  He died to make us good,
That we might go at last to heaven,
  Saved by his precious blood.
There was no other good enough
  To pay the price of sin;
He only could unlock the gate
  Of heaven, and let us in.

3 Oh, dearly, dearly has he loved,
  And we must love him too,
And trust in his redeeming blood,
  And try his works to do.
For there's a green hill far away,
  Without a city wall,
Where the dear Lord was crucified,
  Who died to save us all.

Mrs. Cecil F. Alexander.

SONGS OF CHRIST.

WONDROUS LOVE.   S. F. ACKLEY.

1. Oh my Saviour, how I love thee, Thou did'st shed thy blood for me,
Thou did'st give thy life to save me, Naught will I withhold from thee.

CHORUS.
Wondrous love that seal'd my pardon, Wondrous love that makes me free;
Wondrous love that died for sinners, Teach me, Lord, to love like thee.

Copyright, 1891, by Hunt & Eaton.

77

2 Blessed Jesus, how I love thee,
  Mind, and strength, and heart, and soul,
Help me tell the wondrous story,
  How thy power hath made me whole.

3 Oh my Saviour, how I love thee,
  Never was a love like thine;
Thou hast purchased my redemption,
  I am saved by love divine.

4 Oh my Saviour, how I love thee,
  For salvation full and free;

All my life shall be devoted
  Unto him who died for me.

5 Oh my Saviour, how I love thee,
  Thou dost smile from heaven above,
Thou dost guide me by thy Spirit,
  Thou dost fill with perfect love.

6 Blessed Saviour, how I love thee,
  How I bless thee and adore;
Source of life, and light, and loving,
  Teach me, Lord, to love thee more.

Maggie E. Gregory.

SONGS OF CHRIST.

MASTER, THE TEMPEST IS RAGING.

H. R. Palmer.

1. Mas-ter, the tempest is rag-ing! The billows are toss-ing high! The sky is o'er-shad-owed with black-ness, No shel-ter or help is nigh; "Car-est thou not that we per-ish?" How canst thou lie a-sleep, When each mo-ment so mad-ly is threat'ning A grave in the an-gry deep?

CHORUS.

The winds and the waves shall o-bey thy will, Peace, be still! Peace, be still! peace, be still!

Copyright, 1874, in Songs of Love.

MASTER, THE TEMPEST IS RAGING.—*Concluded.*

78

2 Master, with anguish of spirit
   I bow in my grief to-day;
The depths of my sad heart are troubled—
   Oh, waken and save, I pray!
Torrents of sin and of anguish
   Sweep o'er my sinking soul;
And I perish! I perish! dear Master—
   Oh, hasten, and take control!—Cho.

3 Master, the terror is over,
   The elements sweetly rest;
Earth's sun in the calm lake is mirrored,
   And heaven's within my breast;
Linger, O blessed Redeemer!
   Leave me alone no more;
And with joy I shall make the blest harbor,
   And rest on the blissful shore.—Cho.

Mary A. Baker.

SONGS OF CHRIST.

WELCOME, JESUS, WELCOME.
Frank L. Armstrong.

1. In the ark most holy, Once the Lord appear'd, There to bless his people, Who his mandate fear'd; Wheresoe'er this symbol Found a resting place, There were sweetest tokens, Of Jehovah's grace.

CHORUS. Welcome, Jesus, welcome, Welcome to my heart, Make it now thy dwelling-place, And never more depart, Make it now thy dwelling-place, And never more depart.

From "The Helper," by permission.

79

2 Now God's chosen temple,
   Where he will impart
Heaven's richest blessings,
   Is my sinful heart;
At the door he's knocking,
   Waiting to come in,—
Welcome, Jesus, welcome,
   Cleanse my heart from sin.—Cho.

3 Wheresoever Jesus
   Is a welcome guest,
In the heart or household,
   There is sweetest rest;
Welcome, blessed Saviour,
   Show me now thy grace,
Make my heart thy temple,
   Thine own dwelling-place.—Cho.
         Rev. J. B. Atchinson.

SONGS OF CHRIST.

80

1 We for his sake count all things loss;
   On earthly good look down;
And joyfully sustain the cross,
   Till we receive the crown.—Cho.

3 O let us stir each other up,
   Our faith by works to approve,
By holy, purifying hope,
   And the sweet task of love.—Cho.

4 Let all who for the promise wait,
   The Holy Ghost receive;
And, raised to our unsinning state,
   With God in Eden live.—Cho.

5 Live, till the Lord in glory come,
   And wait his heaven to share:
He now is fitting up your home;
   Go on, we'll meet you there.—Cho.

Charles Wesley

SONGS OF CHRIST.

GRATEFUL PRAISE.—*Concluded.*

81

2 The dearest gifts of heaven,
  Love's written word of truth;
To us is early given
  To guide our steps in youth.
We hear the wond'rous story,—
  The tale of Calvary;
We read of homes in glory,
  From sin and sorrow free.—Cho.

3 Redeemer, grant thy blessing,
  Oh, teach us how to pray;
That each, thy fear possessing,
  May tread life's onward way.
Then where the pure are dwelling,
  We hope to meet again;
And sweeter numbers swelling,
  Forever praise thy name.—Cho.

Harriet Phillips.

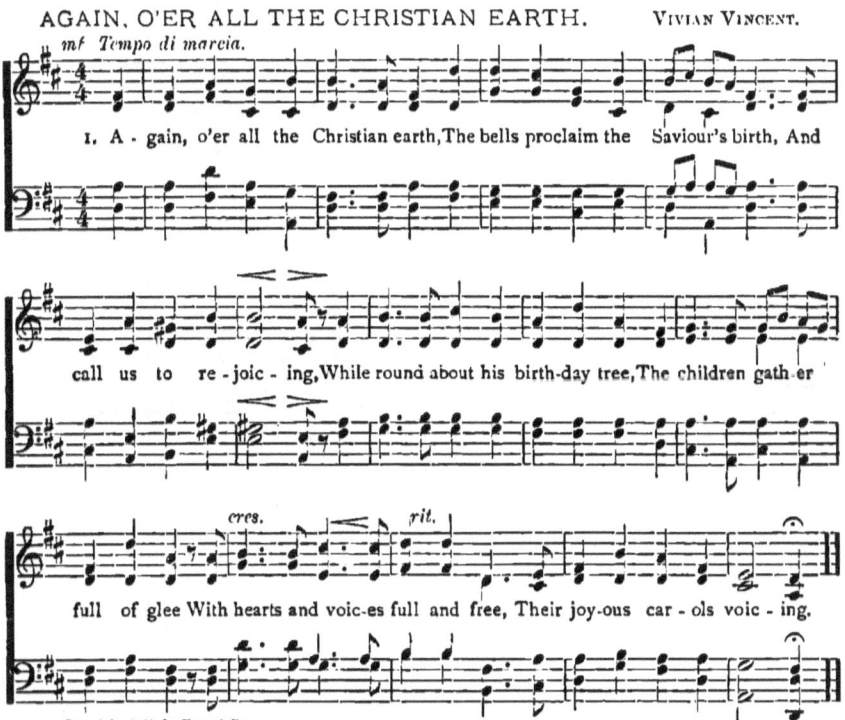

AGAIN, O'ER ALL THE CHRISTIAN EARTH. VIVIAN VINCENT.

1. A-gain, o'er all the Christian earth, The bells proclaim the Saviour's birth, And call us to re-joic-ing, While round about his birth-day tree, The children gath-er full of glee With hearts and voic-es full and free, Their joy-ous car-ols voic-ing.

Copyright, 1891, by Hows & Eaton.

82

2 O earth! forget the chill and frost,
Forget the treasures thou hast lost,
  And still thy winds' repining:
The fir-tree and the cedar come
To decorate both church and home,
  All bright with hearts that beat as one
    Where green festoons are turning.

3 O hearts! forget the ills of life,
Forget the toil and care and strife.
  The sorrow and repining!
And see again, by Fancy's aid,
The Baby in the manger laid,
Adored by Shepherds sore afraid,—
  And Star of Bethlehem shining!

Lilian Grey.

SONGS OF CHRIST.

JESUS CALLS THEE.

THEO. E. PERKINS.

1. Thy sins I bore on Calvary's tree; The stripes thy due were laid on me, That peace and par-don might be free, O wretch-ed sin-ner come to me.

CHORUS.

O sin-ner come, sin-ner come, 'Tis Je-sus calls thee, sin-ner come.

Copyright, 1891, by Theo. E. Perkins.

83

2 O'erwhelmed with guilt, wouldst thou be blest?
Trust not the world; it gives no rest:
I bring relief to hearts opprest
O weary sinner, come to me.—CHO.

3 Come leave thy burden at the cross;
Count all thy gains but empty dross,
My grace repays all earthly loss—
O needy sinner, come to me.—CHO.

4 Come, hither bring thy boding fears,
Thy aching heart, thy flowing tears,
'Tis mercy's voice salutes thine ears;
O trembling sinner, come to me.—CHO.

THE SONG OF SALVATION.

S. V. R. FORD.

1. Once when the world lay a-wea-ry Un-der the king-dom of wrong;

Copyright, 1901, by Hunt & Eaton.

SONGS OF CHRIST.

THE SONG OF SALVATION.—*Concluded.*

84

2 Up from the slumbering ages,
  All through the years gone by,
Swelleth the song that the angels
  Sang to the earth and sky;
Song of a world's salvation,
  Wonderful now as then:
" Glory to God in the highest,
  Peace, and good-will to men."—Cho.

3 Now from the loftiest temple,
  Now from the lowliest home;
Over the world's wide borders,
  Up through the heaven's blue dome;
Ringeth the song of redemption,
  Blessing where sorrow hath been:
" Glory to God in the highest,
  Peace, and good-will to men! "—Cho.

Mary B. Toucey.

SONGS OF CHRIST.

THE ANGELS' STORY.

ROBERT L. FLETCHER.

1. Angels tell the joyful story Of the resurrection day;
They alone beheld the glory When the bars of death gave way;
Hear them saying: "He is risen; Seek him not among the dead;"
They beheld the empty prison, Death in chains was captive led,
Hear them saying: "He is risen; Seek him not among the dead;"

Copyright, 1890, by Robert L. Fletcher.

SONGS OF CHRIST.

THE ANGELS' STORY.—*Concluded.*

85

2 Sing his praises, O ye mortals,
  Strew the earth with vernal flowers;
Jesus passes through death's portals,
  Rises o'er its gloomy powers;
Angel guards the way attending,
  Lo, he goes to dwell on high;
Seraphs there, before him bending,
  Chant his praises in the sky.

3 Gracious Saviour, live forever,
  Victor o'er the prince of night;
And from thee no power can sever
  What is thine by blood-bought right:
Thine the kingdom, thine the glory,
  Fairest of the heavenly train;
Ours the joy to wait before thee,
  Till we rise with thee to reign.
                                  R. L. F.

ABBA, FATHER.   Theo. E. Perkins.

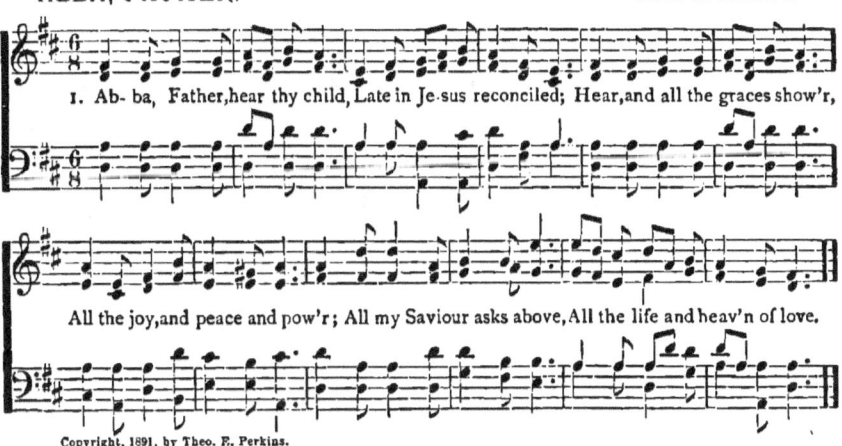

Copyright, 1891, by Theo. E. Perkins.

86

2 Lord, I will not let thee go
  Till the blessing thou bestow:
  Hear my Advocate divine;
  Lo! to his my suit I join;
  Joined to his, it cannot fail;
  Bless me, for I will prevail.

3 Heavenly Father, Life divine,
  Change my nature into thine;
  Move, and spread throughout my soul,
  Actuate, and fill the whole:
  Be it I no longer now
  Living in the flesh, but thou.

4 Holy Ghost, no more delay;
  Come, and in thy temple stay:
  Now thine inward witness bear,
  Strong, and permanent, and clear:
  Spring of life, thyself impart;
  Rise eternal in my heart.
                            Charles Wesley.

SONGS OF CHRIST.

THE TRIUMPH-SONG.

Robert L. Fletcher.

2 For his great redemption,
  By the cross he bore,
Come with praise before him,
  Worship and adore;
Hasten thus his kingdom,
  O'er the earth begun,
Spreading from the rising
  To the setting sun.—Ref.

3 Shrink not back nor falter,
  Ye who serve the King;
Christ, the mighty Conqu'ror,
  Will deliverance bring;
Sing your Leader's triumphs,
  Holy Church of God;
Follow in the foot-prints
  Of the path he trod.—Ref.

4 On this day of battle,
  Rise and meet the foe;
Clad in heavenly armor,
  Christians, forward go;
Forward with your banners,
  Spoil the hosts of wrong;
Christians, on to vict'ry,
  Raise the triumph-song.—Ref.

R. L. F.

SONGS OF THE HOLY SPIRIT.

GERAR. S. M. *Moderato.* — Lowell Mason.

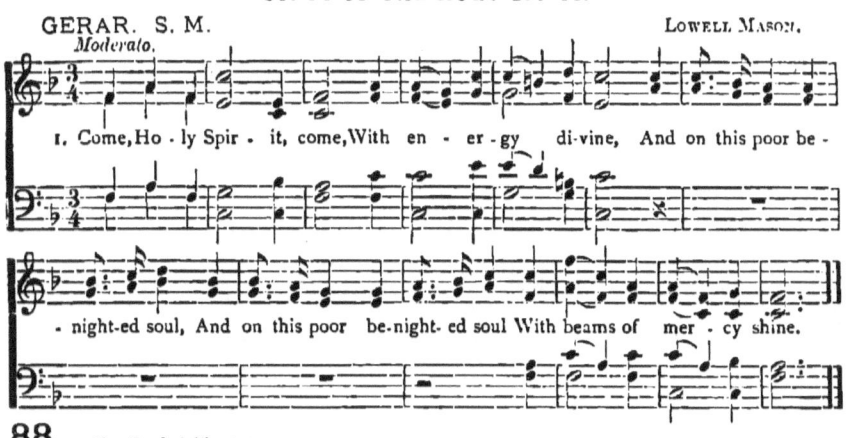

1. Come, Ho-ly Spir-it, come, With en-er-gy di-vine, And on this poor be-night-ed soul, And on this poor be-night-ed soul With beams of mer-cy shine.

88 *For the Spirit's energy.*

2 From the celestial hills
Light, life, and joy dispense;
And may I daily, hourly, feel
Thy quickening influence.

3 O melt this frozen heart,
This stubborn will subdue;

Each evil passion overcome,
And form me all anew.

4 The profit will be mine,
But thine shall be the praise,
Cheerful to thee will I devote
The remnant of my days.

Benjamin Beddome

WOLHAYES 7s. *Cheerful.*

1. Thou, who cam-est from a-bove, Bring-ing light and breath-ing love, Teach-ing us thy per-fect way, Giv-ing gifts to men to-day. A-men.

89 *Praise to the Trinity.*

2 Thou, who once did change our state
Making us regenerate,
Help us evermore to be
Faithful subjects unto thee.

3 Often have we grieved thee sore;
May we never grieve thee more;
Thou the feeble canst protect,
Thou the wandering direct.

4 We are dark; be thou our light;
We are blind; be thou our sight;
Be our Comfort in distress;
Guide us through the wilderness.

5 Praise the blessed Three in One,
Praise the Father and the Son;
To the Holy Ghost arise
Praise from all below the skies!

SONGS OF THE HOLY SPIRIT.

1. Come, Holy Spirit, raise our songs To reach the wonders of that day, When, with thy fiery cloven tongues Thou didst such glorious scenes display.

90 *Pentecostal gifts.*

2 Lord, we believe to us and ours,
  The apostolic promise given;
We wait the pentecostal powers,
  The Holy Ghost sent down from heaven.

3 Assembled here with one accord,
  Calmly we wait the promised grace,
The purchase of our dying Lord;
  Come, Holy Ghost, and fill the place.

4 If every one that asks, may find,
  If still thou dost on sinners fall,
Come as a mighty rushing wind;
  Great grace be now upon us all.

5 O leave us not to mourn below,
  Or long for thy return to pine;
Now, Lord, the Comforter bestow,
  And fix in us the Guest divine.

Charles Wesley.

OUR BLEST REDEEMER, ERE HE BREATHED. J. B. DYKES.

1. Our blest Redeemer, ere he breathed His tender, last farewell, A Guide, a Comforter bequeathed, With us to dwell.

91

2 He came, sweet influence to impart,
  A gracious, willing Guest,
While he can find one humble heart
  Wherein to rest.

3 And every virtue we possess,
  And every victory won,
And every thought of holiness
  Is his alone.

Miss Harriet Auber.

SONGS OF THE SCRIPTURES.

GIVE ME THE BIBLE. P. M.
E. S. Lorenz.

1. Give me the Bi - ble, star of glad - ness gleam-ing, To cheer the wand.'rer lone and temp-est-tossed; No storm can hide that radiance peaceful beam - ing, Since Je - sus came to seek and save the lost. Give me the Bi - ble! ho - ly mes-sage shin - ing, Thy light shall guide me in the nar - row way.

D. S.—Pre - cept and prom - ise, law and love com-bin - ing, Till night shall van - ish in e - ter - nal day.

Copyright, 1883, by E. S. Lorenz.

92

2 Give me the Bible, when my heart is broken,
    When sin and grief have filled my soul with fear;
  Give me the precious words by Jesus spoken,
    Hold up faith's lamp to show my Saviour near.—Cho

3 Give me the Bible, all my steps enlighten,
    Teach me the danger of these realms below;
  That lamp of safety, o'er the gloom shall brighten,
    That light alone the path of peace can show.—Cho.

4 Give me the Bible, lamp of life immortal,
    Hold up that splendor by the open grave;
  Show me the light from heaven's shining portal,
    Show me the glory gilding Jordan's wave.—Cho.

Priscilla J. Owens.

SONGS OF THE SCRIPTURES.

THE LEAVES OF LIFE.

W. J. Kirkpatrick.

Copyright, 1890, by C. R. Blackall, for W. J. Kirkpatrick.

93

1 Ye winds that once by Chebar's flood
   With heavenly breath reviv'd the slain,
Blow earthward from the trees of God,
   And strew their golden leaves again.

2 Ye streams from Zion's mountain sides,
   These gifts that from her gardens fall,
Bear swiftly on your shining tides,
   And love's free blessing yield for all.

3 Ye birds of peace, to men who meet
   In strife, or toss in tempest, bring

The olive sprays, evangels sweet,
   And tell the kindness of the King

4 Stay not, ye heralds of his grace,
   His tidings glad to send abroad,
Till dying souls in every place
   Arise, the ransomed sons of God.

5 Salvation's song from grief shall wake,
   Where drop these leaves of life divine,
His holy words whose pow'r can make
   The face of death like morning shine.
                              Rev. Theron Brown.

DALLAS. 7s.   From Maria Luigi Cherubini.

94   *Holy Bible.*

1 Holy Bible, book divine,
   Precious treasure, thou art mine;
Mine to tell me whence I came;
Mine to teach me what I am.

2 Mine to chide me when I rove;
Mine to show a Saviour's love;
Mine thou art to guide and guard;
Mine to punish or reward;

3 Mine to comfort in distress,
   Suffering in this wilderness;
Mine to show, by living faith,
Man can triumph over death;

4 Mine to tell of joys to come,
   And the rebel sinner's doom:
O thou holy book divine,
Precious treasure, thou art mine.
                              John Burton.

SONGS OF THE SCRIPTURES.

HOLY BIBLE, WELL I LOVE THEE.

G. F. Root.

1. Holy Bible, well I love thee: Thou didst shine upon my way,
Like the glorious sun above me, Turning darkness into day.

CHORUS.
Just as the sun rolls back the night, Breaking forth with morning ray,
So does the Bible's spreading light, Chase the shades of sin away.

95

2 Holy Bible, mines of treasure
In thy precious folds I see;
Earthly good would know no measure
If this world were ruled by thee.
CHORUS.
Just as the sun, from morn till noon,
Stately climbs the eastern sky,
So over all the earth shall soon
Beam the Day-spring from on high.

3 Holy Bible, thou wilt cheer me
When I lay me down to die;
Christ has promised to be near me:—
Can I fear when he is nigh?
CHORUS.
Just as the sun descends at eve,
Soon with fresher beams to rise,
So shall the dying saint receive
Life eternal in the skies.

Author unknown

SONGS OF THE SCRIPTURES.

WHAT GLORY GILDS THE SACRED PAGE. Arr. by A. S. Sullivan.

96 *Glory of the Scriptures.*

1 What glory gilds the sacred page!
  Majestic, like the sun,
It gives a light to every age;
  It gives, but borrows none.
The power that gave it still supplies
  The gracious light and heat;
Its truths upon the nations rise:
  They rise, but never set.

2 Lord, everlasting thanks be thine
  For such a bright display,
As makes a world of darkness shine
  With beams of heavenly day.
My soul rejoices to pursue
  The steps of him I love,
Till glory breaks upon my view
  In brighter worlds above.

William Cowper.

SONGS OF SALVATION.

HARK, MY SOUL! IT IS THE LORD.
S. V. R. Ford.

Copyright, 1891, by Hunt & Eaton.

97   *Love to the Saviour.*

2 "I delivered thee when bound,
And, when bleeding, healed thy wound;
Sought thee wandering, set thee right,
Turned thy darkness into light.

3 "Can a mother's tender care
Cease toward the child she bare?
Yes, she may forgetful be,
Yet will I remember thee.

4 "Mine is an unchanging love,
Higher than the heights above;
Deeper than the depths beneath,
Free and faithful, strong as death.

5 "Thou shalt see my glory soon,
When the work of faith is done;
Partner of my throne shalt be;
Say, poor sinner, lov'st thou me?"

William Cowper. Ab.

I BRING MY SINS TO THEE.

S. V. R. Ford.

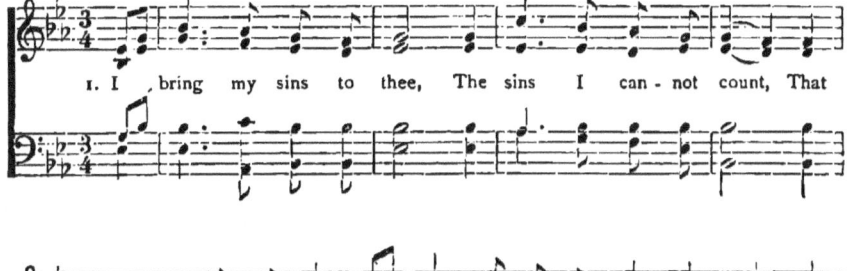

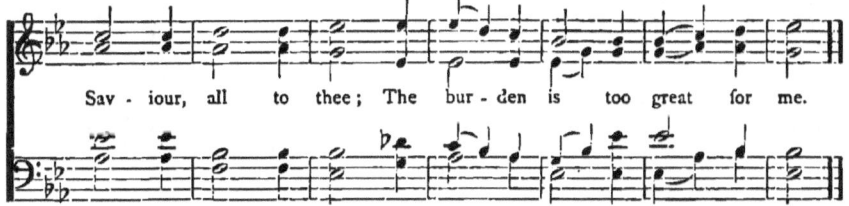

Copyright, 1891, by Hunt & Eaton.

98

1 I bring my sins to thee,
 The sins I cannot count,
That all may cleansed be
 In thy once opened fount.
I bring them, Saviour all to thee;
The burden is too great for me.

2 My heart to thee I bring,
 The heart I cannot read,
A faithless, wand'ring thing,
 An evil heart indeed.
I bring it, Saviour, now to thee,
That fixed and faithful it may be.

3 I bring my grief to thee,
 The grief I cannot tell;
No words shall needed be,
 Thou knowest all so well.
I bring the sorrow laid on me,
O suffering Saviour, all to thee.

4 My joys to thee I bring,
 The joys thy love has given,
That each may be a wing
 To lift me nearer heaven.
I bring them, Saviour, all to thee,
Who hast procured them all for me.

5 My life I bring to thee,
 I would not be my own:
O Saviour, let me be
 Thine ever, thine alone!
My heart, my life, my all I bring
To thee, my Saviour and my King.

Frances Ridley Havergal.

SONGS OF SALVATION.

I BRING MY SINS TO THEE.   S. V. R. FORD.

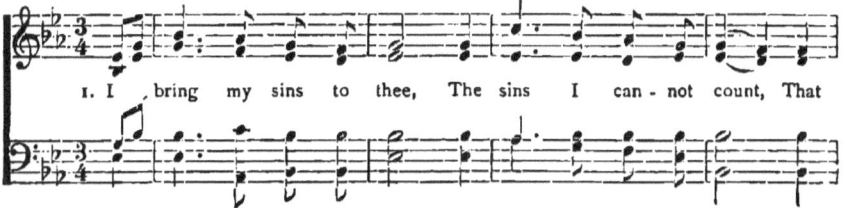

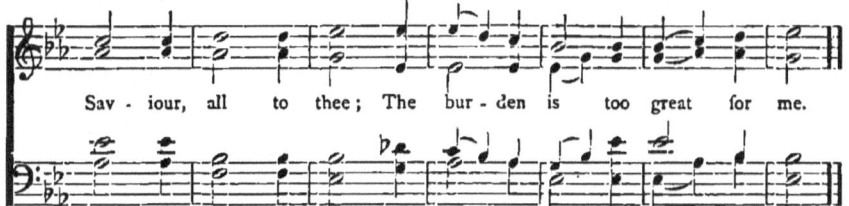

Copyright, 1891, by Hunt & Eaton.

98

1 I bring my sins to thee,
  The sins I cannot count,
That all may cleansed be
  In thy once opened fount.
I bring them, Saviour all to thee;
The burden is too great for me.

2 My heart to thee I bring,
  The heart I cannot read,
A faithless, wand'ring thing,
  An evil heart indeed.
I bring it, Saviour, now to thee,
That fixed and faithful it may be.

3 I bring my grief to thee,
  The grief I cannot tell;
No words shall needed be,
  Thou knowest all so well.
I bring the sorrow laid on me,
O suffering Saviour, all to thee.

4 My joys to thee I bring,
  The joys thy love has given,
That each may be a wing
  To lift me nearer heaven.
I bring them, Saviour, all to thee,
Who hast procured them all for me.

5 My life I bring to thee,
  I would not be my own:
O Saviour, let me be
  Thine ever, thine alone!
My heart, my life, my all I bring
To thee, my Saviour and my King.
                Frances Ridley Havergal.

SONGS OF SALVATION.

HOW TO WIN.

S. F. Ackley.

1. If you feel a love for sin-ners, Do not cold and i-dle stand,
Though you have no words to ut-ter, You can reach a friend-ly hand.
Give a grasp that's kind and earn-est, It will sure-ly reach the heart,
It may help some friendless wand-'rer, To ac-cept the bet-ter part.

CHORUS.
Con-se-crate your all to Je-sus, Give the hand, the heart, the voice;

SONGS OF SALVATION.

HOW TO WIN.—Concluded.

99

2 Never look upon the sinner,
    With a cold and scornful eye;
Just remember what compassion,
    Jesus showed in days gone by.

Let your glance be kind and winning,
    Let it show the love you feel
For the sinful ones that Jesus
    Came to bless, and save, and heal.
            Lanta Wilson Smith.

SAVIOUR, I COME TO THEE.   S. V. R. Ford.

100

2 I come to thee for peace!
    The curse of sin lies heavy on my soul;
But thou canst cause to cease   [roll.
    The thunders of the law that round me

3 I come to thee for light!
    For all the flickering tapers of the earth
Cannot illume the night   [birth.
    That hangs about the spirit from its

4 I come to thee for rest!
    For oft I faint and weary by the way;

Calm thou the troubled breast,
    And give me glimpses of the coming day.

5 I come to thee for strength!
    I feel I'm weak—I cannot go alone;
And so I seek at length   [throne
    The aid proceeding downward from thy

6 I come to thee for all!   [come;
    To comfort me if sorrow's hour should
To rouse me when I fall,
    To fit me here for yonder heavenly home.
            Anonymous.

SONGS OF SALVATION.

HARK! THE VOICE OF JESUS CALLING.
H. R. Palmer, by per.

101 *The Call of the Disciples.*

2 Who will heed the holy mandate,
  "Follow me, follow me!"
Leaving all things at his bidding,
  "Follow, follow me!"
Hark! that tender voice entreating
  Mariners on life's rough sea,
Gently, lovingly, repeating,
  "Follow, follow me!"

3 Hearken, lest he plead no longer,
  "Follow me, follow me!"
Once again, oh, hear him calling,
  "Follow, follow me!"
Turning swift at thy sweet summons,
  Evermore, O Christ, would we,
For thy love all else forsaking,
  Follow, follow thee!

Mary B. Sleight.

TO-DAY THE SAVIOUR CALLS.
Lowell Mason.

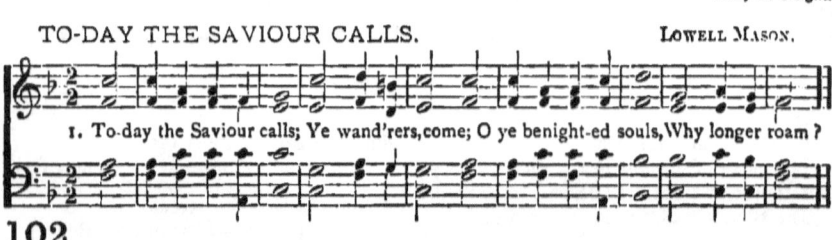

102

2 To-day the Saviour calls;
  O hear him now;
Within these sacred walls
  To Jesus bow.

3 To-day the Saviour calls;
  For refuge fly;

The storm of justice falls,
  And death is nigh.

4 The Spirit calls to-day;
  Yield to his power;
O grieve him not away,
  'Tis mercy's hour.

S. F. Smith, D.D.

SONGS OF SALVATION.

JESUS IS MIGHTY TO SAVE. Frank M. Davis.

Copyright in "Scriptural Songs" used by permission.

103

1 When in the tempest he'll hide me,
  When in the storm he'll be near,
All the way long he will carry us on
  So now we have nothing to fear.—Cho.

2 When in my sorrow he found me,
  Found me, and bade me be whole,
Turned all my night into heavenly light
  And from me my burdens did roll.—Cho.

3 Why are you doubting and fearing,
  Why are you still under sin? [abound?
Have you not found that his grace doth
  He's mighty to save! let him in!—Cho.

SONGS OF SALVATION.

YES, JESUS IS MIGHTY TO SAVE.

W<small>M</small>. G. F<small>ISCHER</small>, by per.

104

1 All glory to Jesus be given,
That life and salvation are free;
And all may be washed and forgiven,
And Jesus can save even me.

2 From the darkness and sin and despair,
Out into the light of his love,
He has brought me, and made me an heir,
To kingdoms and mansions above.

3 Oh, the rapturous heights of his love,
The measureless depths of his grace;
My soul all his fullness would prove,
And live in his loving embrace.

4 In him all my wants are supplied,
His love makes my heaven below,
And freely his blood is applied,
His blood that makes whiter than snow.

Mrs. Annie Wittenmyer.

SONGS OF SALVATION.

105

1 Christ is knocking at my sad heart;
  Shall I let him in?
Patiently pleading with my sad heart;
  Oh! shall I let him in?
Cold and proud is my heart with sin;
Dark and cheerless is all within;
Christ is bidding me turn unto him,
  Oh! shall I let him in?

2 Shall I send him the loving word;
  Shall I let him in?
Meekly accepting my gracious Lord;
  Oh! shall I let him in?

He can infinite love impart;
He can pardon this rebel heart;
Shall I bid him forever depart,
  Or shall I let him in?

3 Yes, I'll open this heart's proud door,
  Yes, I'll let him in;
Gladly I'll welcome him evermore;
  Oh! yes, I'll let him in.
Blessed Saviour, abide with me;
Cares and trials will lighter be;
I am safe if I'm only with thee,
  Oh! blessed Lord, come in.

H. R. Palmer.

SONGS OF SALVATION.

CALLING, PLEADING, WAITING.

S. V. R. Ford.

1. The Sav-iour is call-ing, O sin-ner for thee, The voice of his love whis-pers, "Come un-to me!" The blest in-vi-ta-tion no long-er de-spise, De-lay not one mo-ment, make haste to be wise.

REFRAIN.
Call-ing for thee, for thee, Je-sus is call-ing, O sin-ner for thee;
Call-ing for thee, for thee, Je-sus is call-ing, O sin-ner for thee.

Copyright, 1891, by Hunt & Eaton.

CALLING, PLEADING, WAITING.—*Concluded.*

106

2 The Saviour is pleading, O sinner with thee
To taste of his mercy, so boundless and free,
He purchased thy ransom with sorrow and pain,
And still he entreats thee to love him in vain.

3 The Saviour is waiting, O sinner for thee,
He asks thy decision, O what shall it be?
Spurn, spurn not his presence, say not: "Go thy way!"
Lest grieving the Spirit, thou perish for aye.

S. V. R. F.

ONLY TRUST HIM.

Rev. J. H. Stockton, by per.

1. Come, ev-'ry soul by sin oppress'd, There's mercy with the Lord, And he will sure-ly give you rest, By trust-ing in his word.

CHORUS. On-ly trust him, on-ly trust him, On-ly trust him now; He will save you, he will save you, He will save you now.

107

2 For Jesus shed his precious blood
Rich blessings to bestow;
Plunge now into the crimson flood
That washes white as snow.—Cho.

3 Yes, Jesus is the Truth, the Way,
That leads you into rest;
Believe in him without delay,
And you are fully blest.—Cho.

4 Come then, and join this holy band,
And on to glory go,
To dwell in that celestial land,
Where joys immortal flow.—Cho.

Rev. J. H. S.

SONGS OF SALVATION.

THE SAVIOUR CALLS.—*Concluded.*

108

1 The Saviour calls in accents clear,
And in compassion now draws near;
My brother, hear that pleading voice,
And make eternal life your choice.—REF.

2 If you this dearest Friend refuse,
And proffered mercy still abuse,
No hope will cheer the journey's end,
When you the vale of death descend.—REF.

3 But if you trust his constant care,
He will your soul for heaven prepare;
Support you in the whelming flood,
And bear you safe to his abode.—REF.

4 The golden moments pass in haste,
And leave your life a dreary waste;
Regain this hour the lost estate,
For death and judgment on thee wait.–REF.

R. L. F.

I WILL FOLLOW THEE.

J. H. ROSECRANS.

Copyright, 1890, by Fillmore Bros.

109

1 Jesus, I will follow thee,
For I hear thee calling me,
Loving, trusting, glad I come,
To let thee lead me home.—CHO.

2 Little eyes might loose the way,
Little feet might go astray,

I might weak and weary be,
But thou art strong for me.—CHO.

3 Grief and want may be my foes,
Foolish sins my way oppose,
Full of courage I will be,
Whene'er I follow thee.—CHO.

Grace Glenn

SONGS OF SALVATION.

SEEK MY SOUL.
Geo. Wm. Warren.
Lento non troppo.

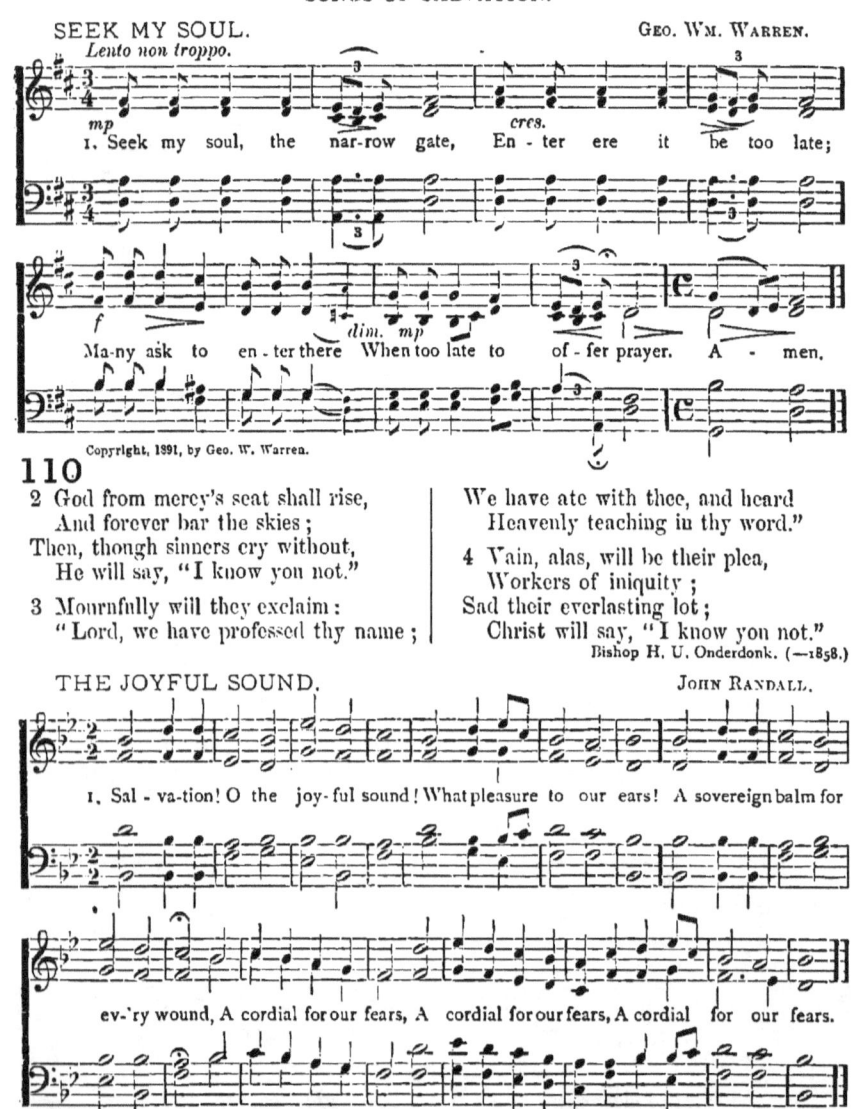

1. Seek my soul, the nar-row gate, En-ter ere it be too late; Ma-ny ask to en-ter there When too late to of-fer prayer. A-men.

Copyright, 1891, by Geo. W. Warren.

110

2 God from mercy's seat shall rise,
And forever bar the skies;
Then, though sinners cry without,
He will say, "I know you not."

3 Mournfully will they exclaim:
"Lord, we have professed thy name;
We have ate with thee, and heard
Heavenly teaching in thy word."

4 Vain, alas, will be their plea,
Workers of iniquity;
Sad their everlasting lot;
Christ will say, "I know you not."
Bishop H. U. Onderdonk. (—1858.)

THE JOYFUL SOUND.
John Randall.

1. Sal-va-tion! O the joy-ful sound! What pleasure to our ears! A sovereign balm for ev-'ry wound, A cordial for our fears, A cordial for our fears, A cordial for our fears.

111

2 Salvation! let the echo fly
The spacious earth around,
While all the armies of the sky
Conspire to raise the sound.

3 Salvation! O thou bleeding Lamb!
To thee the praise belongs:
Salvation shall inspire our hearts,
And dwell upon our tongues.
Isaac Watts.

JESUS CHRIST IS PASSING BY.

112

1 Jesus Christ is passing by,
Sinner lift to him thine eye ;
As the precious moments flee,
Cry, be merciful to me !

2 Lo ! he stands and calls to thee,
"What wilt thou then have of me?"
Rise, and tell him all thy need ;
Rise, he calleth thee indeed.

3 "Lord, I would thy mercy see ;
Lord, reveal thy love to me ;
Let it penetrate my soul,
All my heart and life control."

4 Oh, how sweet the touch of power
Comes,—and is salvation's hour :
Jesus gives from guilt release,
"Faith hath saved thee, go in peace !"
J. Denham Smith.

TO THEE I COME.

113
By permission.

2 Jesus, I come—I cannot stay
From thee another precious day ;
I would thy word at once obey—
   Jesus, to thee I come !
   Jesus, to thee I come !

3 Jesus, I come—"just as I am,"
To thee, the holy, spotless Lamb ;
Thou wilt receive me as I am—
   Jesus, to thee I come !
   Jesus, to thee I come !
Anon.

SONGS OF SALVATION.

GOD LOVED THE WORLD OF SINNERS LOST. Wm. G. Fischer.

1. God loved the world of sinners lost, And ruined by the fall;
Salvation full, at highest cost, He offers free to all.

CHORUS.
Oh, 'twas love, 'twas wondrous love! The love of God to me;
It brought my Saviour from above, To die on Calvary.

114

2 Ev'n now by faith I claim him mine,
  The risen Son of God;
Redemption by his death I find,
  And cleansing thro' the blood.—Cho

3 Love brings the glorious fullness in,
  And to his saints makes known
The blessed rest from inbred sin,
  Thro' faith in Christ alone.—Cho

4 Believing souls, rejoicing go;
  There shall to you be given
A glorious foretaste, here below,
  Of endless life in heaven.—Cho.

5 Of victory now o'er Satan's power
  Let all the ransomed sing,
And triumph in the dying hour
  Thro' Christ the Lord our King.—Cho.

Mrs. Martha M. Stockton.

SONGS OF SALVATION.

ONCE FOR ALL THE SAVIOUR DIED. T. C. O'KANE.

1. Once for all the Saviour died, Christ the Lord was crucified;
Once for all he shed his blood, Bearing forth a purple flood.

REFRAIN.
O, believe him and be blest! O, receive him and find rest!
All your sins shall be forgiv'n, You shall reign with him in heav'n.

Copyright, 1881, by T. C. O'Kane.

115

2 Once for all our sins he bore,
Bought our peace for evermore;
Once for all our debt he paid,
Full, complete atonement made.—REF

3 Once for all the Saviour rose,
Victor o'er his mighty foes;
With the glorious King and Head,
Saints shall waken from the dead.—REF.

4 Once for all ascending high,
Throned and crowned above the sky,
There he intercedes and reigns—
Praise him in triumphant strains.—REF.

Rev. J. H. Martin.

SONGS OF SALVATION.

NOW BLESS ME.
WM. J. KIRKPATRICK.

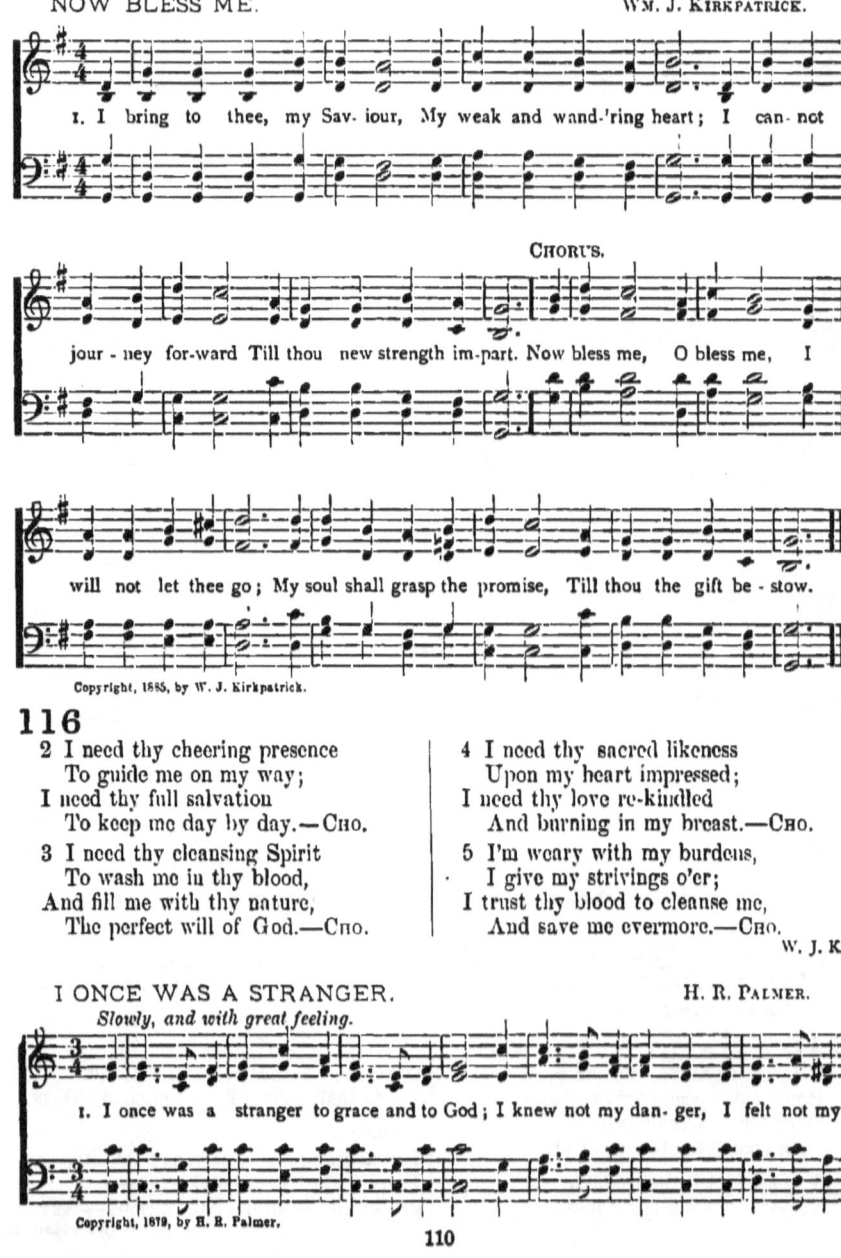

1. I bring to thee, my Saviour, My weak and wand-'ring heart; I can-not jour-ney for-ward Till thou new strength im-part. Now bless me, O bless me, I will not let thee go; My soul shall grasp the promise, Till thou the gift be-stow.

Copyright, 1885, by W. J. Kirkpatrick.

116

2 I need thy cheering presence
To guide me on my way;
I need thy full salvation
To keep me day by day.—CHO.

3 I need thy cleansing Spirit
To wash me in thy blood,
And fill me with thy nature,
The perfect will of God.—CHO.

4 I need thy sacred likeness
Upon my heart impressed;
I need thy love re-kindled
And burning in my breast.—CHO.

5 I'm weary with my burdens,
I give my strivings o'er;
I trust thy blood to cleanse me,
And save me evermore.—CHO.

W. J. K.

I ONCE WAS A STRANGER.
H. R. PALMER.

Slowly, and with great feeling.

1. I once was a stranger to grace and to God; I knew not my dan-ger, I felt not my

Copyright, 1879, by H. R. Palmer.

SONGS OF SALVATION.

I ONCE WAS A STRANGER.—*Concluded.*

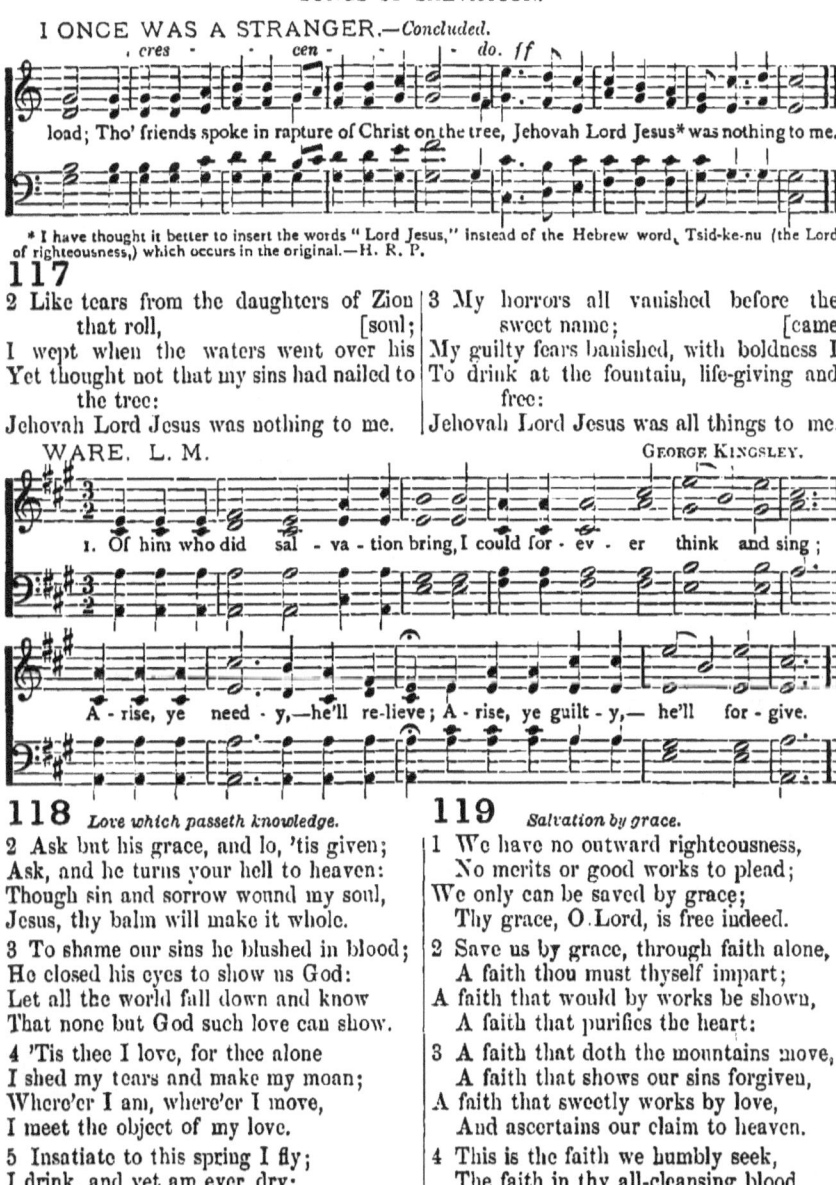

load; Tho' friends spoke in rapture of Christ on the tree, Jehovah Lord Jesus* was nothing to me.

* I have thought it better to insert the words "Lord Jesus," instead of the Hebrew word, Tsid-ke-nu (the Lord of righteousness,) which occurs in the original.—H. R. P.

117

2 Like tears from the daughters of Zion that roll, [soul;
I wept when the waters went over his
Yet thought not that my sins had nailed to the tree:
Jehovah Lord Jesus was nothing to me.

3 My horrors all vanished before the sweet name; [came
My guilty fears banished, with boldness I
To drink at the fountain, life-giving and free:
Jehovah Lord Jesus was all things to me.

WARE. L. M.   GEORGE KINGSLEY.

1. Of him who did sal - va - tion bring, I could for - ev - er think and sing;
A - rise, ye need - y,—he'll re-lieve; A - rise, ye guilt - y,— he'll for - give.

118 *Love which passeth knowledge.*

2 Ask but his grace, and lo, 'tis given;
Ask, and he turns your hell to heaven:
Though sin and sorrow wound my soul,
Jesus, thy balm will make it whole.

3 To shame our sins he blushed in blood;
He closed his eyes to show us God:
Let all the world fall down and know
That none but God such love can show.

4 'Tis thee I love, for thee alone
I shed my tears and make my moan;
Where'er I am, where'er I move,
I meet the object of my love.

5 Insatiate to this spring I fly;
I drink, and yet am ever dry:
Ah! who against thy charms is proof?
Ah! who that loves, can love enough?
    Bernard of Clairvaux. Tr. by A. W. Boehm.

119 *Salvation by grace.*

1 We have no outward righteousness,
No merits or good works to plead;
We only can be saved by grace;
Thy grace, O Lord, is free indeed.

2 Save us by grace, through faith alone,
A faith thou must thyself impart;
A faith that would by works be shown,
A faith that purifies the heart:

3 A faith that doth the mountains move,
A faith that shows our sins forgiven,
A faith that sweetly works by love,
And ascertains our claim to heaven.

4 This is the faith we humbly seek,
The faith in thy all-cleansing blood,
That blood which doth for sinners speak;
O let it speak us up to God!
    Charles Wesley.

SONGS OF SALVATION.

HAMBURG. L. M.   Gregorian Chant. Arr. by Lowell Mason.

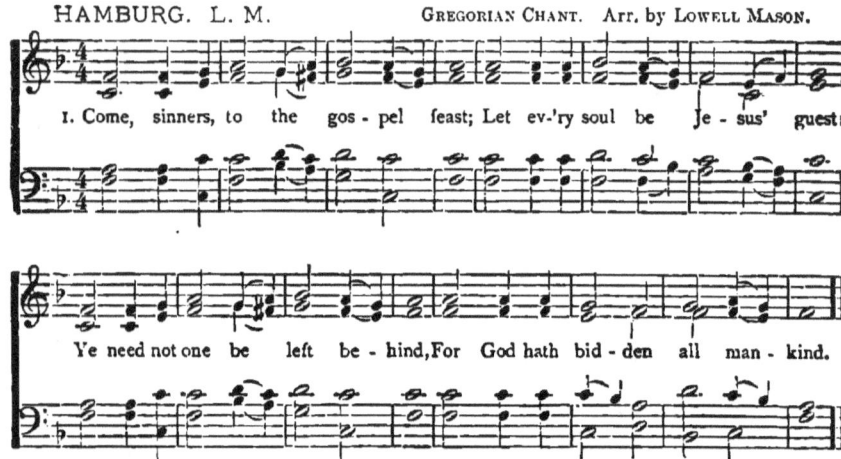

1. Come, sinners, to the gos-pel feast; Let ev-'ry soul be Je-sus' guest;
Ye need not one be left be-hind, For God hath bid-den all man-kind.

120 *The gospel feast.*

2 Sent by my Lord, on you I call;
The invitation is to all:
Come all the world! come, sinner, thou,
All things in Christ are ready now.

3 Come, all ye souls by sin oppressed,
Ye restless wanderers after rest;
Ye poor, and maimed, and halt, and blind,
In Christ a hearty welcome find.

4 My message as from God receive;
Ye all may come to Christ and live:
O let his love your hearts constrain,
Nor suffer him to die in vain.

5 See him set forth before your eyes,
That precious, bleeding sacrifice:
His offered benefits embrace,
And freely now be saved by grace.
                       Charles Wesley.

WHILE JESUS WHISPERS TO YOU.   H. R. Palmer.

1. While Je-sus whispers to you, Come, sin-ner come; While we are pray-ing for you, Come, sin-ner, come. Now is the time to own him,

Copyright, 1879, by H. R. Palmer.

SONGS OF SALVATION.

WHILE JESUS WHISPERS TO YOU.—*Concluded.*

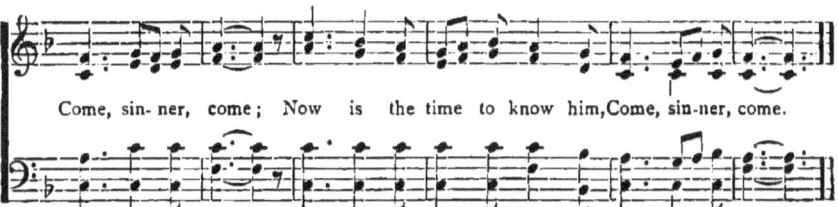

Come, sin-ner, come; Now is the time to know him, Come, sin-ner, come.

121

2 Are you too heavy laden?
Come, sinner, come;
Jesus will bear your burden,
Come, sinner, come.
Jesus will not deceive you,
Come, sinner, come;
Jesus can now redeem you,
Come, sinner, come.

3 Oh, hear his tender pleading,
Come, sinner, come;
Come, and receive the blessing,
Come, sinner, come.
While Jesus whispers to you,
Come, sinner, come;
While we are praying for you,
Come, sinner, come.
Will. E. Witter.

LUTON. L. M. Rev. George Burder.

1. Ho! ev-'ry one that thirsts draw nigh: 'Tis God in-vites the fall-en race:
Mer-cy and free sal-va-tion buy; Buy wine, and milk, and gos-pel grace.

122 *The abundance of his grace.*

1 Ho! every one that thirsts draw nigh:
'Tis God invites the fallen race:
Mercy and free salvation buy;
Buy wine, and milk, and gospel grace.

2 Come to the living waters, come!
Sinners, obey your Maker's call;
Return, ye weary wanderers, home,
And find his grace is free for all.

3 See from the Rock a fountain rise;
For you in healing streams it rolls;
Money ye need not bring, nor price,
Ye laboring, burdened, sin-sick souls.

4 Nothing ye in exchange shall give;
Leave all you have and are behind;
Frankly the gift of God receive;
Pardon and peace in Jesus find.
John Wesley

1 Teach me, O Lord, by faith alone,
  Thy perfect will to prove;
And know the pow'r of Christ to atone,
  And fill me with his love.
Though I am sinful, all defiled,
  No light, nor love within;
Yet God can make me his own child,
  And cleanse me from all sin.—Ref.

2 Help me, O Lord, life's journey through,
  To live with "single eye;"
In all I think, or speak, or do,
  Thy name to glorify.
So shall I walk in holy love,
  Through Jesus' power given;
Till faith is lost in sight above,
  Among the blest in heaven.—Ref.

C. E. R.

SONGS OF SALVATION.

PRAISE THE LORD FOR HIS LOVE TO ME.
Wm. J. Kirkpatrick.

1. O how hap-py are they, Who the Saviour o-bey And have laid up their treasure a-bove! Tongue can nev-er express The sweet comfort and peace Of a soul in its ear-li-est love.

REFRAIN.
Praise the Lord, praise the Lord, O, my soul, rejoice and sing; Praise the Lord for his love to me. He redeem'd me with his blood, O, the precious, cleansing flood. Hallelu-jah, praise the Lord.

Copyright, 1887, by Wm. J. Kirkpatrick.

124 *The joys of conversion.*

2 That sweet comfort was mine,
  When the favor divine
I received through the blood of the Lamb;
  When my heart first believed,
  What a joy I received,
What a heaven in Jesus's name!—Ref.

3 'Twas a heaven below
  My Redeemer to know,
And the angels could do nothing more
  Than to fall at his feet,
  And the story repeat,
And the Lover of sinners adore.—Ref.

4 Jesus all the day long
  Was my joy and my song:
O that all his salvation might see!
  "He hath loved me," I cried,
  "He hath suffered and died,
To redeem even rebels like me."—Ref.

5 O the rapturous height
  Of that holy delight
Which I felt in the life-giving blood!
  Of my Saviour possessed,
  I was perfectly blessed,
As if filled with the fullness of God.—Ref.

Charles Wesley.

SONGS OF SALVATION.

I'M KNEELING AT THE DOOR.

T. E. Perkins, by per.

125

1 I'm kneeling, Lord, at mercy's gate,
   With trembling hope and fear;
I've waited long, and still I wait
   Thy gracious voice to hear.
Thy precious word has bid me seek
   The joys thou hast in store.—Cho.

2 None ever empty turned away,
   Who truly sought thy face:
And I, my Saviour, come to-day,
   To seek thy pardoning grace.
Thy precious blood is all my plea:
   This can my soul restore.—Cho.

Mrs. Lydia C. Baxter.

SONGS OF SALVATION.

DIVINE UNION. Mrs. Joseph F. Knapp.

126

1 Who can unfold the bliss untold,
 Dear Saviour, found in thee?
 The rapturous love they daily prove
 Who only Jesus see.—Cho.

2 To live alone for thee—our own
 Redeemer—so adored!
 To do and bear each word and care,
 For thee, most blessed Lord!—Cho.

3 Oh, hallowed bliss—no joy like this,
 Unfailing, sweet, and pure!—
 Thy love to know in ceaseless flow,
 And feel it will endure.—Cho.

4 Thy radiant face, thy matchless grace,
 Jesus—thou fairest One,—
 To earth have given the joys of heaven!
 With thee 'tis heaven begun!—Cho.

Mary D. James.

SONGS OF SALVATION.

HE HAS COME.—*Concluded.*

127

2 He has come! He has come! My Love and my Lord,
Every thought of my being is swayed by his word;
He has come! and he rules in the realms of my soul,
And his scepter is love, O blessed control!—Cho.

3 He has come! He has come! O happiest heart,
He has given his word that he will not depart;
No trouble can enter, no evil can come,
To the heart where the God of peace has his home.—Cho

4 He has come to abide, and holy must be
The place where my Lord deigns to banquet with me;
And this is my prayer, Lord, since thou art come,
Make meet for thy presence my heart as thy home.—Cho.

Mrs. J. H. Knowles.

ONE HARMONIOUS CHORUS. Arr. by L. Mason.

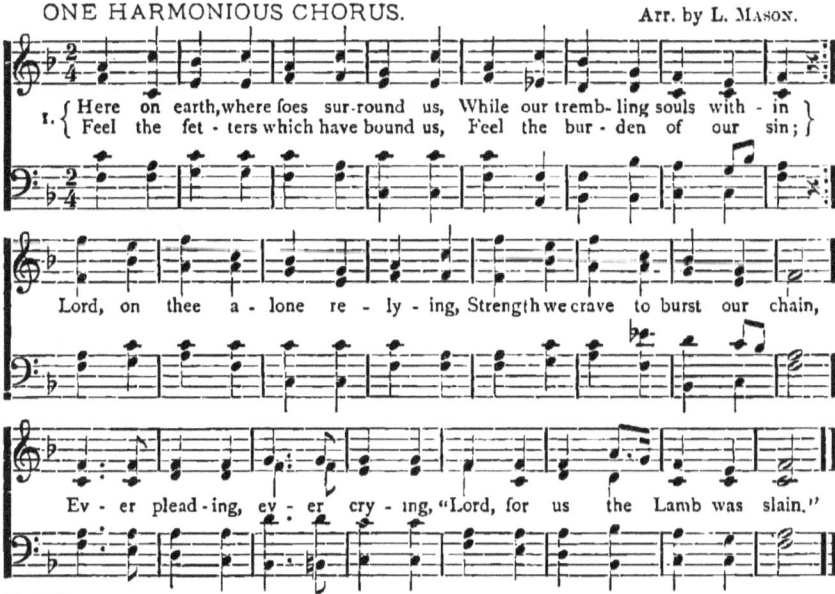

1. { Here on earth, where foes sur-round us, While our tremb-ling souls with-in }
   { Feel the fet-ters which have bound us, Feel the bur-den of our sin; }
Lord, on thee a-lone re-ly-ing, Strength we crave to burst our chain,
Ev-er plead-ing, ev-er cry-ing, "Lord, for us the Lamb was slain."

128 *The harmonious chorus.*

2 In those high and holy regions
 Where the blest thy praise prolong,
Cherubs and seraphic legions
 Know no theme of nobler song;
White-robed saints, who there adore thee
 Throned above the glassy main,
Sing, and cast their crowns before thee,
 "Lord, for us the Lamb was slain."

3 Thus thy Church, whate'er her dwelling
 Heaven above or earth below,
One harmonious chorus swelling,
 Loves her Saviour's praise to show:
Here in trial, there in glory,
 Changeless rings the immortal strain,
Changeless sounds the wondrous story,
 "Lord, for us the Lamb was slain."

Unknown.

SONGS OF SALVATION.

THE SAVIOUR BIDS THEE COME.--*Concluded.*

129

2 Strait is the gate, and narrow
   The way that leads to life;
But, oh! what great salvation,
   That ends the sinful strife.
What joy and peace unbounded
   Possess the new-born soul;
What rest, what blissful freedom,
   When made entirely whole!—Cho.

3 The race by sin is blinded,
   And have not ears to hear;
Rejecting love and mercy,
   With scarce a thought or fear
And yet the Spirit calleth,
   And points the heav'nly road,
That leads to joys immortal,
   Close by the throne of God.—Cho.

C. E. Rowley.

JESUS CALLING.

Rev. Albert Gould.

1. How sweetly sounds the call, The Saviour gives to all, "Come unto me;" Though faint and weary, come, With all thy burdens come, With trusting hearts, still come, Here's rest for thee.

Copyright, 1891, by Hunt & Eaton.

130

2 When weary in the way,
   O hear the Saviour say;
"Come unto me;"
Bring all thy doubts and fears;
Bring all thy griefs and tears;
The feeblest cry he hears:
   There's rest for thee.

3 Rest for the weary heart,
   To us O Lord impart,
   We come to thee;
Grant us thy love to know;
On us thy grace bestow;
May each one here below
   Find rest in thee.

L. E. Hitchcock.

SONGS OF SALVATION.

WINCHESTER OLD. C. M. — Thomas Este's Psalter.

1. O what amazing words of grace Are in the gospel found! Suited to ev-'ry sinner's case, Who knows the joyful sound.

131 *Full and free.*

2 Poor, sinful, thirsty, fainting souls
Are freely welcome here;
Salvation, like a river, rolls
Abundant, free, and clear.

3 Come, then, with all your wants and
Your every burden bring: [wounds;
Here love, unchanging love, abounds,
A deep celestial spring.

4 Whoever will—O gracious word!
May of this stream partake;
Come, thirsty souls, and bless the Lord
And drink, for Jesus' sake.

5 Millions of sinners, vile as you,
Have here found life and peace;
Come, then, and prove its virtues too,
And drink, adore, and bless.

Samuel Medley, alt.

LISBON. S. M. — Daniel Read.

1. And can I yet delay My little all to give? To tear my soul from earth away For Jesus to receive?

132 *The surrender.*

2 Nay, but I yield, I yield;
I can hold out no more:
I sink, by dying love compelled,
And own thee conqueror.

3 My one desire be this,
Thy only love to know;

To seek and taste no other bliss,
No other good below.

4 My life, my portion thou;
Thou all-sufficient art:
My hope, my heavenly treasure, now
Enter, and keep my heart.

Charles Wesley.

SONGS OF SALVATION.

HE WAS NOT WILLING.
LUCY RIDER MEYER.

1. "He was not willing that any should perish;" Jesus enthron'd in the glory above, Saw our poor fall-en world, pit-ied our sorrows, Pour'd out his life for us— won-der-ful love! Per-ish-ing, per-ish-ing! Throng-ing our path-way, Hearts break with bur-dens too hea-vy to bear,

D.S.—Jesus would save, but there's no one to tell them, No one to lift them from sin and de-spair.

Copyright, 1889, by Lucy Rider Meyer.

133

2 "He was not willing that any should perish;"
Cloth'd in our flesh with its sorrow and pain,
Came he to seek the lost, comfort the mourner,
Heal the heart, broken by sorrow and shame.
Perishing, perishing! harvest is passing,
Reapers are few and the night draweth near;
Jesus is calling thee, haste to the reaping,
Thou shalt have souls, precious souls for thy hire.

3 Plenty for pleasure, but little for Jesus;
Time for the world, with its troubles and toys,
No time for Jesus' work, feeding the hungry,
Lifting lost souls to eternity's joys.
Perishing, perishing! hark, how they call us:
"Bring us your Saviour, oh, tell us of him!
We are so weary, so heavily laden,
And with long weeping our eyes have grown dim.
Lucy Rider Meyer.

SONGS OF SALVATION.

DELAYING TO COME.   D. B. TOWNER.

1. Thou, O sinner! art delaying, Yield unto the Spirit's pow'r,
Others all around are praying, Come to Christ this very hour.
With your conscience you are trifling, Even while you now delay,
Deep convictions you are stifling, Do not wait another day.

Copyright, 1888, by D. B. Towner.

134

2 Are you certain of the morrow,
    That you falter thus and wait?
Coming time you cannot borrow,
    Trifling, you may seal your fate;
Come at once and do not linger,
    While the Master calls for thee,
Scorn may point the taunting finger,
    But the Lord will set you free.

3 Tho' your sins may rise like mountains,
    Cutting off your soul from God,
Yet his grace, in healing fountains,
    Flows by faith in Jesus' blood;
Sinner, then delay no longer,
    For more feeling do not wait,
Feeling may not grow the stronger,
    Waiting, you may be too late.
                  T. Whiting Bancroft.

SONGS OF SALVATION.

SINNER, WHAT SAY YOU?   Rev. Samuel Alman.

Copyright, 1891, by Hunt & Eaton.

135

2 Reveille has sounded
  At the early dawn,
Calling us to duty.
  Now the day is done—
As we light our camp-fires
  'Neath the falling dew,
Can we say we've conquered?
  Sinner, what say you?

3 When life's war is ended,
  And the setting sun
Marks our last day's battle,
  And we're going home,
What will be our greeting
  In that land of light?
Sinner, are you ready
  To go home to-night?

Geneva G. Moore

SONGS OF SALVATION.

BOAST NOT OF TO-MORROW.—*Concluded.*

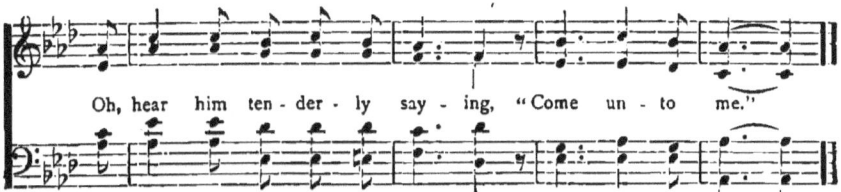

Oh, hear him ten-der-ly say-ing, "Come un-to me."

136

2 "Boast not thyself of to-morrow,"
  For brittle is life's thread;
  What if that day should disclose thee
  Among the silent dead?—Cho.

3 "Boast not thyself of to-morrow,"
  Nor trust to mercy's guise;
  To-day is radiant with promise,
  And bids thy soul be wise.—Cho.

4 "Boast not thyself of to-morrow,"
  Its hopes delusive are;
  The passing moments are hastening
  The night of deep despair.—Cho.

5 "Boast not thyself of to-morrow,"
  Death waits for one and all,
  While time to thee is extended,
  On Christ, the Saviour, call.—Cho.

  R. L. F.

I WILL SEEK THE LORD TO-DAY.

C. B. WIKEL.

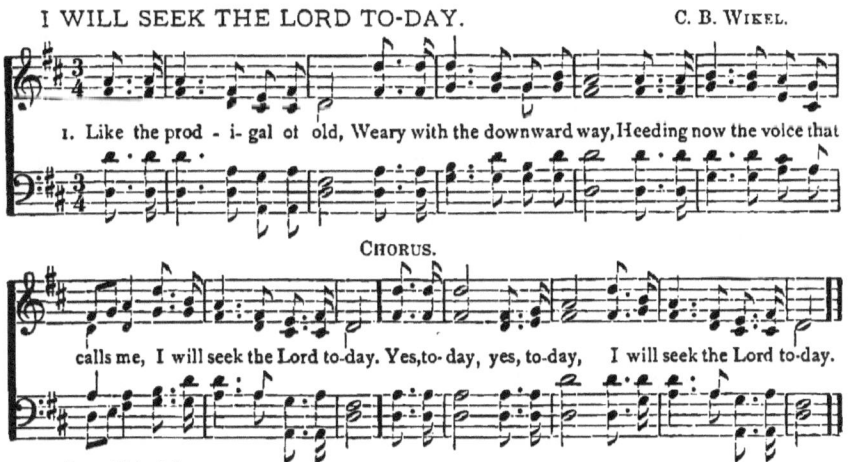

1. Like the prod-i-gal of old, Weary with the downward way, Heeding now the voice that calls me, I will seek the Lord to-day. Yes, to-day, yes, to-day, I will seek the Lord to-day.

By per. W. A. Ogden.

137

2 With my load of guilt and sin,
  That he waits to take away,
  Knowing that his blood can cleanse me,
  I will seek the Lord to-day.—Cho.

3 That his love may fill my soul,
  And his light illume my way,

  Looking to the cross before me,
  I will seek the Lord to-day.—Cho.

4 That his hand may lead me on
  Through the perils of my way,
  Knowing that he died to save me,
  I will seek the Lord to-day.—Cho.

  E. A. Bar .

SONGS OF SALVATION.

THE GREAT PHYSICIAN.   Arr. by Rev. J. H. Stockton.

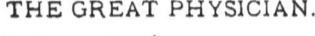

1. The great Physician now is near, The sympathizing Jesus: He speaks the drooping heart to cheer, Oh, hear the voice of Jesus.

CHORUS.

Sweetest note in seraph song, Sweetest name on mortal tongue, Sweetest carol ever sung, Jesus, blessed Jesus.

138

2 Your many sins are all forgiven,
　Oh, hear the voice of Jesus;
Go on your way in peace to heaven,
　And wear a crown with Jesus.

3 All glory to the dying Lamb!
　I now believe in Jesus;
I love the blessed Saviour's name,
　I love the name of Jesus.

4 The children too, both great and small,
　Who love the name of Jesus,
May now accept the gracious call
　To work and live for Jesus.

5 Come, brethren, help me sing his praise,
　Oh, praise the name of Jesus;
Come, sisters, all your voices raise,
　Oh, bless the name of Jesus.

6 His name dispels my guilt and fear,
　No other name but Jesus;
Oh, how my soul delights to hear
　The precious name of Jesus.

7 And when to that bright world above,
　We rise to see our Jesus,
We'll sing around the throne of love
　His name, the name of Jesus.

Anon.

SONGS OF THE CHRISTIAN LIFE.

THE ROCK THAT IS HIGHER THAN I.   WM. G. FISCHER.

1. O, sometimes the shadows are deep, And rough seems the path to the goal, And sorrows, sometimes how they sweep Like tempests down over the soul.

CHORUS.
Oh, then, to the Rock let me fly, To the Rock that is higher than I; Oh, then, to the Rock let me fly, To the Rock that is higher than I.

By permission.

139

2 Oh, sometimes how long seems the day,
And sometimes how weary my feet;
But toiling in life's dusty way,
The Rock's blessed shadow, how sweet!

3 Oh, near to the Rock let me keep,
Or blessings, or sorrows prevail;
Or climbing the mountain-way steep,
Or walking the shadowy vale.

E. Johnson.

SONGS OF THE CHRISTIAN LIFE.

TELL IT TO JESUS ALONE. P. M.   E. S. Lorenz.

Copyright, 1880, by E. S. Lorenz, by per.

140

2 Do the tears flow down your cheeks unbidden?
Tell it to Jesus, tell it to Jesus.
Have you sins that to man's eye are hidden?
Tell it to Jesus alone.

3 Do you fear the gathering clouds of sorrow?
Tell it to Jesus, tell it to Jesus.
Are you anxious what shall be to-morrow?
Tell it to Jesus alone.

4 Are you troubled at the thought of dying?
Tell it to Jesus, tell it to Jesus.
For Christ's coming kingdom are you sighing?
Tell it to Jesus alone.

J. E. Rankin, D.D.

SONGS OF THE CHRISTIAN LIFE.

I WANT A HEART TO PRAY.

Copyright, 1891, by Theo. E. Perkins.

141

2 I want a true regard,
  A single, steady aim,
Unmoved by threatening or reward,
  To thee and thy great name;
A jealous, just concern
  For thine immortal praise;
A pure desire that all may learn
  And glorify thy grace.

3 I rest upon thy word;
  The promise is for me;
My succor and salvation, Lord,
  Shall surely come from thee:
But let me still abide,
  Nor from my hope remove,
Till thou my patient spirit guide
  Into thy perfect love.

Charles Wesley.

SONGS OF THE CHRISTIAN LIFE.

REFUGE.
Robert L. Fletcher.

1. Whenever trials press my soul, And clouds, like angry seas that roll, Conceal God's face from mine;
I still shall trust his constant care, And to the throne of grace repair, To plead for help divine.

Used by per. of Robert L. Fletcher, owner of Copyright.

142

2 Whene'er temptations throng the way,
And Satan's host in dread array,
   Conspire to do me harm;
For refuge, Lord, I'll turn to thee,
That my protection then may be
   Thine everlasting arm.

3 When storms arise and fears invade,
And there is found no shelt'ring shade,
   I'll trust in thee, O God!

Dear refuge from the foes unseen,
O let my soul in trouble lean
   For comfort on thy rod.

4 And when the trials and the strife,
That mock the fleeting years of life,
   All end with death's embrace;
My soul shall take its lofty flight,
To dwell with God, where all is light,
   And see him face to face.

MARCHING TO ZION.
Will. S. Fitch.

1. Chil-dren of the heav'nly king, As we jour-ney sweetly sing; Sing our Saviour's wor - thy praise, Glorious in his works and ways.

REFRAIN.
We're marching, we're marching,
We're marching, marching, marching, march.

Copyrighted, 1879, in *Song Leaflet*, by Rev. W. S. Fitch.

SONGS OF THE CHRISTIAN LIFE.

MARCHING TO ZION. *Concluded.*

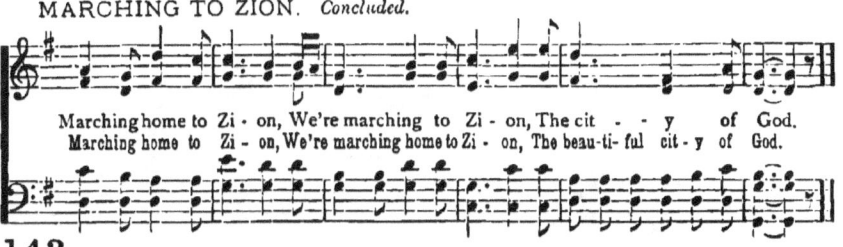

Marching home to Zi - on, We're marching to Zi - on, The cit - - y of God.
Marching home to Zi - on, We're marching home to Zi - on, The beau-ti-ful cit - y of God.

143

2 We are trav'ling home to God,
In the way our fathers trod;
They are happy now, and we
Soon their happiness shall see.—REF.

3 Fear not, brethren, joyful stand
On the borders of our land;
Jesus Christ, our Father's Son,
Bids us undismayed go on.—REF.

John Cennick.

ROCKPORT. 7s, 6s, 8.　　　　　ISAAC BAKER WOODBURY.

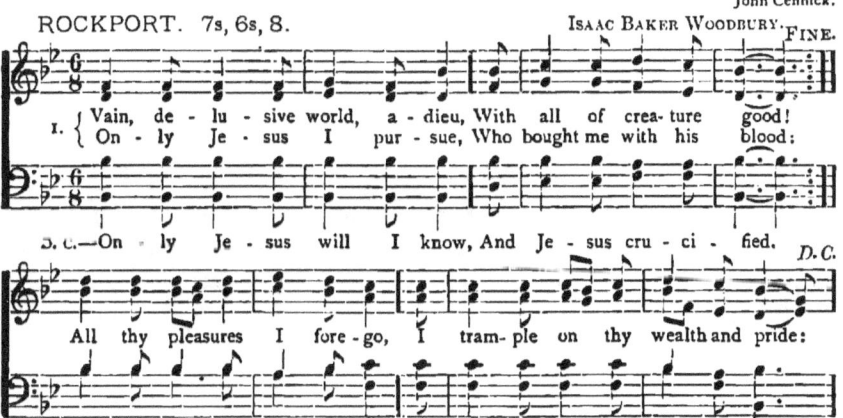

1. { Vain, de - lu - sive world, a - dieu, With all of crea - ture good!
   { On - ly Je - sus I pur - sue, Who bought me with his blood;
D. C.—On - ly Je - sus will I know, And Je - sus cru - ci - fied.
All thy pleasures I fore - go, I tram - ple on thy wealth and pride:

144　*Nothing but Christ crucified.*

2 Other knowledge I disdain;
'Tis all but vanity:
Christ, the Lamb of God, was slain,
He tasted death for me.
Me to save from endless woe
The sin-atoning Victim died:
Only Jesus will I know,
And Jesus crucified.

3 Here will I set up my rest;
My fluctuating heart
From the haven of his breast
Shall never more depart:
Whither should a sinner go?
His wounds for me stand open wide;
Only Jesus will I know,
And Jesus crucified.

4 Him to know is life and peace,
And pleasure without end;
This is all my happiness,
On Jesus to depend;
Daily in his grace to grow,
And ever in his faith abide;
Only Jesus will I know,
And Jesus crucified.

5 O that I could all invite,
This saving truth to prove;
Show the length, the breadth, the height,
And depth of Jesus' love!
Fain I would to sinners show
The blood by faith alone applied:
Only Jesus will I know,
And Jesus crucified.

Charles Wesley.

145

1 Ever looking upward, as a trusting child,
I would follow Jesus, meek and mild;
I would serve the Master, doing what I may
In the world's great vineyard all the while I stay.—Cho

2 Ever looking foward, full of hope and youth,
I would join the workers in the cause of Truth,
Looking out, not inward, wide-awake I stand,
Ready for each duty with a willing hand.—Cho.

SONGS OF THE CHRISTIAN LIFE.

WHERE HE LEADS I'LL FOLLOW.

W. A. Ogden.

146

2 Sweet is the tender love Jesus hath shown;
Sweeter far than any love that mortals have known;
Kind to the erring one, faithful is he;
He the great example is, and pattern for me.—Cho.

3 List! to his loving words, "Come unto me,"
Weary, heavy-laden, there is sweet rest for thee;
Trust in his promises, faithful and sure;
Lean upon the Saviour, and thy soul is secure.—Cho.

W. A. Ogden.

SONGS OF THE CHRISTIAN LIFE.

CONSECRATION. Mrs. Joseph F. Knapp.

Copyright, 1869, by Joseph F. Knapp. By per.

147

1 My body, soul and spirit,
  Jesus, I give to thee,
A consecrated offering,
  Thine evermore to be.—Cho.

2 O, Jesus, mighty Saviour,
  I trust in thy great name,
I look for thy salvation,
  Thy promise now I claim.—Cho.

3 O, let the fire descending
  Just now upon my soul,
Consume my humble offering,
  And cleanse and make me whole.—Cho.

4 I am thine, O blessed Jesus,
  Washed by thy cleansing blood;
Now seal me by thy Spirit
  A sacrifice to God.—Cho.

Mary D. James

SONGS OF THE CHRISTIAN LIFE.

IT IS FROM HIM.

S. V. R. Ford.

1. The Lord he is my strength and stay When sorrow's cup o'erflows the brim; It sweet-ens all if I can say, It is from him! it is from him!

148 Copyright, 1891, by Hunt & Eaton.

2 When humbly lab'ring for my Lord
Faint grows the heart and weak the limb,
What strength and joy are in the word,
It is for him! it is for him!

3 I hope forever to abide
Amid the shining seraphim:

Delivered, pardoned, glorified— [him!
But 'tis through him! but 'tis through

4 Then welcome be the hour of death,
When nature's lamp burns low and dim,
If I can cry with dying breath,
I go to him! I go to him!

Charlotte Tucker.

LEIGHTON. C. M.

Greatorex.

1. Sow, ere the eve-ning falls, The seed with-in thy hand, A-long the fur-rows at thy feet, Or broad-cast o'er the land.

149

2 Sow heartfelt deeds and prayers,
Nor question where they lie;
Assured that not the smallest one
Escapes the Master's eye.

3 Sow with no selfish aim,
For soon the time will come.

When he who sifts the chaff from wheat,
Will call his harvest home.

4 Sow all in faith and love;
Though late the gleaning be,
How sweet to hear him say at last,
" Ye did it unto Me."

Mary B. Toucey.

SONGS OF THE CHRISTIAN LIFE.

GO TELL IT TO JESUS. D. B. TOWNER.

Copyright, by D. B. Towner.

150

2 Go tell unto Jesus,
  Thy doubts and thy fears,
Thy sin and thy failures,
  Thy penitent tears;
Thy heart of its trouble
  He'll sweetly relieve,
And whisper, "Beloved,
  Fear not, but believe."—REF.

3 Go tell it to Jesus,
  Whatever befall;
He'll graciously heed it,
  If great or if small:
Cast on him thy burden,
  Whatever it be:
Thou heavily laden,
  He careth for thee.—REF.

Rev. J. H. Sammis, ab.

SONGS OF THE CHRISTIAN LIFE.

GO TELL THE WORLD OF HIS LOVE.

WM. J. KIRKPATRICK.

Copyright, 1895, by W. J. Kirkpatrick.

151

2 Think how he labor'd that we might have rest,
  Go tell the world of his love;
Think how he suffered that we might be bless'd,
  Go tell the world of his love:
Saved by his mercy, upheld by his care,
  Tell of the goodness we constantly share;
Filled with his fulness, no longer forbear,
  Go tell the world of his love.—CHO.

3 Plead with the lost ones to come while they may,
  Go tell the world of his love;
Jesus is waiting, he'll save them to-day,
  Go tell the world of his love:
Love that is nearest when earth-joys are past,
  Lighting our pathway by clouds overcast;
Love that will bring us to glory at last,
  Go tell the world of his love.—CHO.

Abbie Mills.

SONGS OF THE CHRISTIAN LIFE.

DRAW ME TO THEE. W. J. KIRKPATRICK, by per.

152

2 Hope of the desolate
　Light of the soul,
Now of my lonely bark,
　Take thou control.
Yonder the Ark of Grace
　Dimly I see,
Reach out thy loving arm,
　Draw me to thee.—Cho.

3 Lord at the open door
　Let me come in,
Heal thou my broken heart,
　Weary of sin.
Close to thy bleeding side
　Still would I be,
Reach out thy loving arm,
　Draw me to thee.—Cho.

Fanny J. Crosby

SONGS OF THE CHRISTIAN LIFE.

BEST OF ALL.   WM. J. KIRKPATRICK.

Copyright, 1889, by Wm. J. Kirkpatrick.

153

2 Jesus loves and watches o'er me,
When astray he will restore me;
Angel guards he sends before me,
Lest in fatal snares I fall;
With his friends he hath enrolled me,
By his might he will uphold me,
In his arms he will enfold me,
This to me is best of all.
   Best of all, best of all,
     In his arms he will enfold me,
   This to me is best of all.

3 Jesus loves and he will guide me,
All I need he will provide me,
In his bosom he will hide me,
When the woes of life appal;
He will hear my feeblest sighing,
Needful grace to me supplying,
He'll be with me when I'm dying,
This to me is best of all.
   Best of all, best of all,
     He'll be with me when I'm dying,
   This to me is best of all.
                         Rev. C. W. Ray, D.D.

SONGS OF THE CHRISTIAN LIFE.

ALL FOR JESUS. Mrs. Joseph F. Knapp, by per.

154

2 Let my hands perform his bidding,
  Let my feet run in his ways,
  Let my eyes see Jesus only,
  Let my lips speak forth his praise.

REFRAIN.
·||: All for Jesus! all for Jesus!
  Let my lips speak forth his praise. :||:

3 Since my eyes were fixed on Jesus,
  I've lost sight of all beside;
  So enchained my spirit's vision
  Looking at the crucified.

REFRAIN.
:||: All for Jesus! all for Jesus!
  Looking at the crucified. :||:

4 O, what wonder! how amazing!
  Jesus, glorious king of kings,
  Deigns to call me his beloved,
  Lets me rest beneath his wings.

REFRAIN.
:||: All for Jesus! all for Jesus!
  Resting now beneath his wings. :||:

Miss Mary D. James.

SONGS OF THE CHRISTIAN LIFE.

LOOK UP, LIFT UP. Wm. J. Kirkpatrick.

1. Look up to Jesus, lift up thy neighbor, Lead to the Saviour, tell of his power;
Seek for the straying, comfort the weary; Look up for guidance hour by hour,

CHORUS.
Look up, lift up! look up to Jesus, Far above the darkness where his glories shine.
Fill'd with his Spirit, lift up thy neighbor, Then a crown, a glorious crown shall one day be thine.

Copyright, 1891, by Wm. J. Kirkpatrick.

155

1 Look up to Jesus, lift up thy neighbor,
Lead to the Saviour, tell of his power,
Seek for the straying, comfort the weary,
Look up for guidance hour by hour.

2 Look up to Jesus, lift up his banner,
Faithfully follow, stand for the right,
Carry his colors where he may lead you,
Strive for the vict'ry in his might.

3 Look up to Jesus, lift up hosannas,
His hallelujahs ringing above,
Jesus has saved us: let joyful service
Bear grateful witness of his love.

4 Look up to Jesus, lift up a promise,
Trustfully, truly, pray in his name,
For all the erring, make intercession
Look up! a cov'nant blessing claim.

E. E. Hewitt.

SONGS OF THE CHRISTIAN LIFE.

LIVING FOR JESUS.—*Concluded.*

156

2 Heavy the crosses I must bear,
  Many the hours of busy care,—
Jesus has promised all to share,
  While I my journey pursue.—Cho.

3 Lifting his royal standard high,
  Looking to crowns beyond the sky,

Knowing I'll triumph by and by,
  Glad I my journey pursue.—Cho.

4 Swiftly the moments glide along,
  Filling my heart, and hand, and tongue;
Yet with the cheer of prayer and song,
  Do I my journey pursue.—Cho.
                                    Tracy Clinton.

HALLELUJAH! 8s. & 7s.   E. S. LORENZ.

1. Hal-le-lu-jah! song of gladness, Song of ev-er-last-ing joy; Hal-le-lu-jah! song the sweetest That can angel hosts employ. Praise ye the Lord! sing Hallelujah! Praise ye the Lord! sing Hal-le-lu-jah! Praise ye the Lord! sing Hallelujah! Praise ye the Lord!

Copyright, 1886, by E. S. Lorenz.

157 *Praise ye the Lord.*

2 Hallelujah! Church victorious,
  Thou may'st lift this joyful strain;
Hallelujah! songs of triumph
  Well befit the ransomed train.—Cho.

3 Hallelujah! let our voices
  Rise to heaven with full accord;

Hallelujah! every moment
  Brings us nearer to the Lord.—Cho

4 But our earnest supplication,
  Holy God, we raise to thee;
Bring us to thy blissful presence,
  Let us all thy glory see.—Cho.
                                    Anon.

SONGS OF THE CHRISTIAN LIFE.

I AM SHELTERED IN THEE.

FRANK M. DAVIS.

1. I am safe in the Rock that is high-er than I, This my ref-uge thro' storms e'er shall be; Tho' my frail bark is toss'd on the bil-lows' mad foam, Yet I'm shel-ter'd for-ev-er in thee.

CHORUS.

Shel-ter'd in thee, shel-ter'd in thee, in thee, O thou blest Rock of A-ges, I am shelter'd in thee.

¹58

2 I am safe in the Rock that was riven for me,
From the pow'r of the tempter I'm free;
Tho' my pathway be dark and the storms sweep the sky,
Yet securely I'm shelter'd in thee.

3 I am safe in the Rock, let whatever betide,
Death and hell have no terror to me;
I can walk without fear through the shadowy vale,
For securely I'm shelter'd in thee.

F. M. Davis

SONGS OF THE CHRISTIAN LIFE.

SOLDIERS OF THE CROSS ARISE.
S. F. Ackley.

1. Soldiers of the cross arise, Gird you with your armor bright,
Mighty are your enemies, Hard the battle you must fight;
O'er a faithless fallen world, Raise your banner in the sky,
Let it float abroad, unfurled, Bear it onward lifted high.

Copyright, 1891, by Hunt & Eaton.

159

2 'Mid the powers of want and woe,
  Strangers to the living word
Let the Saviour's heralds go,
  Let the voice of hope be heard.
Where the shadows deepest lie,
  Carry truths benignant ray;
Where are crimes of deepest dye,
  There the saving power display

3 To the weary and the worn,
  Tell of realms where sorrows cease;
To the outcast and forlorn,
  Speak of mercy, love and peace.
Keep the banner still unfurled,
  Wield the spirits mighty sword;
Till the kingdoms of the world,
  Are the kingdoms of the Lord.

  Wm. Walsham How.

SONGS OF THE CHRISTIAN LIFE.

LIFT UP THE GOSPEL BANNER.—*Concluded.*

160

2 Lift up the gospel banner,
  Let every sinner see
The path of woe and danger,
  That from it they may flee;
That all may seek their refuge
  In Christ the sinner's friend,
Who only can uphold us,
  And keep us to the end.—Cho.

3 Lift up the gospel banner
  Upon the mountain high,
'Till o'er the earth its glory
  Is seen by every eye;
For Christ shall reign triumphant,
  And all his foes shall fall;
But unto those that love him
  Will he be all in all.—Cho.
      Rev. W. S. Cosner.

BE WITH ME EVERY MOMENT. WM. J. KIRKPATRICK.

1. Be with me ev-'ry mo-ment, Sav-iour mine, Hold thou my trembling hand, Still firm in thine.

REFRAIN.
Be with me ev-'ry mo-ment Of ev-'ry pass-ing hour, And keep me, Sav-iour, keep me By thy un-fail-ing power.

Copyright, 1887, by Wm. J. Kirkpatrick.

161

2 Be with me every moment,
    Day by day,
  Uphold me with thy grace,
    And cheer my way.—Ref.

3 Be with me every moment,
    Blessed One,
  And teach my heart to say,
    Thy will be done.—Ref.

4 In moments of temptation,
    Let me hide
  Within the Rifted Rock,
    And there abide.—Ref.

5 Be with me every moment,
    When I tread
  The silent vale of death,
    Where thou hast led.—Ref.

6 Be with me every moment,
    'Till I rise
  To my eternal home
    Beyond the skies.—Ref.
        Martha J. Lankton.

SONGS OF THE CHRISTIAN LIFE.

I AM RESTING IN THE SAVIOUR'S LOVE.
D. E. Dortch.

From Scriptural Songs, by permission.

163

2 At the fountain opened for the soul unclean,
I am resting in the Saviour's love;
Trusting in his grace I freely ventured in,
I am resting in the Saviour's love.—Ref.

3 All my doubts are vanished, all my foes are gone,
I am resting in the Saviour's love;
When I trusted Jesus, lo! the work was done,
I am resting in the Saviour's love.—Ref.

4 So I live rejoicing in his love to-day,
I am resting in the Saviour's love;
I am walking with him in the narrow way,
I am resting in the Saviour's love.—Ref.

Rev. E. A. Hoffman.

SONGS OF THE CHRISTIAN LIFE.

LEAD ME. WILL. S. FITCH.

1. Lead me, O ef-ful-gent Light, O'er life's dark un-cer-tain way;
Lead me through the realm of night, To the splen-dors of thy day.

REFRAIN.
Lead me, Saviour, all the way; Keep me ev-er at thy side;
Lead me, O lead me all the way; Keep me, O keep me at thy side; Let me, O let me never stray.
Let me never from thee stray; O, with me a-bide.

Copyrighted, 1879, in *Song Leaflet*, by Rev. W. S. Fitch.

164

2 Weak am I, without thy strength;
   Faithless, but for faith from thee;
Blind, yet may my eyes at length,
   Thro' thine own be made to see.—REF.

3 Not a single step alone,
   Can I with assurance take;

Yet with thee, no trembling one
   But it's sure ascent will make.—REF.

4 Step by step, the height shall yield,
   'Till the uttermost is won,
And the restful heavenly field
   Crowns the weary labor done.—REF.

                Mary B. Dodge.

AUREOLA. L. M. S. V. R. Ford.

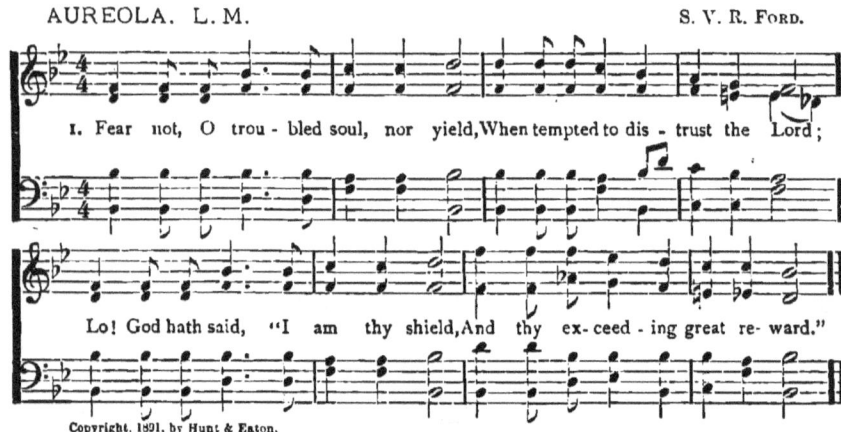

1. Fear not, O trou-bled soul, nor yield, When tempted to dis-trust the Lord;
Lo! God hath said, "I am thy shield, And thy ex-ceed-ing great re-ward."

Copyright, 1891, by Hunt & Eaton.

165 *Fear not, O troubled soul.*

2 Art thou oppressed with poverty?
  Infinite wealth to thee is given;
  But thou must use Faith's golden key
  To unlock the treasury of heaven.

3 Art thou o'erwhelmed with grief or care?
  Thy Father stoops to lift thy load;
  But thou must ask in humble prayer
  This token of his Fatherhood.

4 Doth sin thy quickened conscience sting?
  Christ hath atoned for all thy guilt;
  But, thou must true repentance bring,
  Else 'twere in vain his blood was spilt.

5 All things are thine, yea, more beside:
  Giver and gift, e'en Christ the Lord;
  The Lamb of God—the Crucified—
  Is thy rewarder and reward.

6 Then, fainting soul, be not cast down,
  Though darkness hover o'er thy way;
  Lo! God's eternal light shall crown
  Thy life with its resplendent ray!

  S. V. R. Ford.

DEVIZES. C. M. Isaac Tucker.

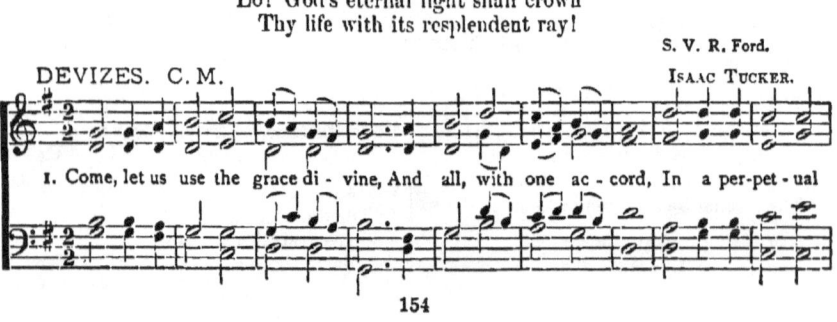

1. Come, let us use the grace di-vine, And all, with one ac-cord, In a per-pet-ual

SONGS OF THE CHRISTIAN LIFE.

DEVIZES.—*Concluded.*

cov-enant join Our-selves to Christ the Lord; Our-selves to Christ the Lord.

166 *Renewing the covenant.*

1 Come, let us use the grace divine,
And all, with one accord,
In a perpetual covenant join
Ourselves to Christ the Lord.

2 Give up ourselves, through Jesus' power,
His name to glorify;
And promise, in this sacred hour,
For God to live and die.

3 The covenant we this moment make
Be ever kept in mind;
We will no more our God forsake,
Or cast his words behind.

4 We never will throw off his fear
Who hears our solemn vow;
And if thou art well pleased to hear,
Come down, and meet us now.

5 Thee, Father, Son, and Holy Ghost,
Let all our hearts receive;
Present with the celestial host,
The peaceful answer give.

6 To each the covenant blood apply,
Which takes our sins away;
And register our names on high,
And keep us to that day.
                            Charles Wesley.

OZREM. S. M.   ISAAC BAKER WOODBURY.

1. Lord, if at thy com-mand The word of life we sow,

Wa-tered by thy al-might-y hand, The seed shall sure-ly grow:

167 *Success certain.*

1 Lord, if at thy command
The word of life we sow,
Watered by thy almighty hand,
The seed shall surely grow:

2 The virtue of thy grace
A large increase shall give,
And multiply the faithful race
Who to thy glory live.

3 Now, then, the ceaseless shower
Of gospel blessings send,
And let the soul-converting power
Thy ministers attend.

4 On multitudes confer
The heart-renewing love,
And by the joy of grace prepare
For fuller joys above.
                            Charles Wesley.

SONGS OF THE CHRISTIAN LIFE.

INVOCATION. (Prayer.)   Sidney Williams.

1. Lord, we come in faith be-liev-ing, That our needs thou wilt sup-ply;
At thy throne as sup-pliants kneel-ing, Grant a bless-ing from on high;
Teach us by thy Ho-ly Spir-it, How to come to thee in pray'r;
At thy feet to cast our bur-dens, Find re-lief from ev-'ry care.

Copyright, 1891, by Robert L. Fletcher.

168   *Prayer.*

2 Consecrate us to thy service;
   From on high our souls endow;
Whither, Saviour, thou dost lead us,
   To thy righteous will we bow;
When assailed by fierce temptations,
   When the storm-clouds darkly lower,
In thy strong pavilion hiding,
   Save and keep us by thy power.

3 Care for those we love and cherish;
   Warm the hearts that now are cold;
Turn the steps of those who wander,
   Back again to seek thy fold;
And, thro' all this world of evil,
   Help thy servants to proclaim
Life and pardon to the sinner
   Thro' the power of thy great name.

4 Draw us, Saviour, draw us nearer;
   Give us grace for every day;
Take away whatever hinders
   When we praise, or talk, or pray;
Fill our hearts with pure devotion;
   May we all this hour partake
Of the fullness of thy blessing;
   All we ask for thy name's sake.

S. W. Arr. by R. L. F.

SONGS OF THE CHRISTIAN LIFE.

YONDER'S MY HOME. H. S. BLUNT.

1. I'm a lonely trav'ller here, Weary, op-press'd; But my journey's end is near, Soon I shall rest. Dark and drear-y is the way, Toil-ing I've come;

CHORUS.
Ask me not with you to stay, Yonder's my home. I'm a trav'ller, call me not, Up-ward I roam; Heaven is my resting place, Yon-der's my home.

Copyright, 1891, by Hunt & Eaton.

169

2 I'm a weary trav'ller here,
　I must go on;
For my journey's end is near,
　I must be gone.
Brighter joys than earth can give,
　Hie me away,
Pleasures that forever live,
　I can not stay.—Cho.

3 I'm a trav'ller to a land
　Where all is fair;
Where is seen no broken band,
　Saints all are there.

Where no tear shall ever fall,
　Nor heart be sad;
Where the glory is for all
　And all are glad.—Cho.

4 I'm a trav'ller, and I go
　Where all is fair;
Farewell all I love below,
　I must be there.
Worldly honors, hopes, and gain,
　All I resign;
Welcome, sorrow, grief, and pain,
　If heaven be mine.—Cho.

JESUS ONLY.

Mrs. Joseph F. Knapp.

1. "Jesus only," is the motto Now engraven on my shield;
Where he leads me I will follow, Fighting bravely on the field.

CHORUS.
Though my heart by sin is tempted, Strong in him I'll never yield;
"Jesus only," is the motto Now engraven on my shield.

170

2 "Jesus only," when I'm doubtful,
  Can my feeble faith make strong;
Only he can wisely counsel, [Cho.
  Make me right where I've been wrong.

3 "Jesus only," his salvation,
  Free and full, and present is;
Thro' his blood I've found redemption,
  Perfect love, deep joy, and bliss.—Cho.

4 "Jesus only," let his praises
  Sound to earth's remotest shore;
Souls from guilt and death he raises,
  Saves them by his mighty power.—Cho.

M. W. L.

SONGS OF THE CHRISTIAN LIFE.

"INASMUCH." LUCY RIDER MEYER.

1. Who is this, a stranger, lying On a low-ly, lone-ly bed? He is suffering, sick and dying—
And for his sake, quickly, gladly, Food and clothing I will bring. *Omit to Refrain.*
Dy-ing for the want of bread. But I look again. O, wonder! 'Tis the brother of my King.

REFRAIN.
And I hear my Sav-ior whis-per, "In-asmuch"—Oh, bless-ed word!—
"All ye do for these my breth-ren, Ye have done to me— the Lord."

Copyright, 1891, by Hunt & Eaton.

171

2 Or his life is spent in darkness,
  In a gloomy prison ward,
Even while the hidden image
  He is bearing of my Lord
I will hasten to the rescue,
  Visit him, so sad and lone,
Knowing that my King I'm serving
  When I feed and clothe his own.—REF.

3 For one day my King—his brother—
  Saw me dying, lost, alone ;
And to save my soul from ruin,
  Gave his life up for my own.

Can I prove that I am grateful
  In a better way than this—
Caring for his helpless brother,
  Helping him in his distress?—REF.

4 O, our blindness! O, for vision!
  Help, Lord, as thy poor we meet,
In the wretched home or hovel,
  In the busy, crowded street—
As we look in stricken faces,
  Thy marred visage still to see,
And to render loving service
  Unto them, as unto thee.—REF.

Cara A. Thomas.

SONGS OF THE CHRISTIAN LIFE.

SING A HYMN TO JESUS.
GEORGE S. WEEKS.

1. Sing a hymn to Jesus, When the heart is faint; Tell it all to Jesus, Comfort or complaint. If the work is sorrow, If the way is long, If thou dread the morrow, Tell it him in song.

CHORUS. *A little faster.*
Sing a hymn to Jesus, When thy heart is faint; Tell it all to Jesus, Comfort or complaint.

Copyright, 1875, by George S. Weeks, by per.

172

2 Jesus, we are lowly,
  Thou art very high;
We are all unholy,
  Thou art purity.
We are frail and fleeting,
  Thou art still the same,
All life's joys are meeting
  In thy blessed name.—CHO.

3 All his words are music,
  Though they make me weep,
Infinitely tender,
  Infinitely deep.

Time can never render
  All in him I see,
Infinitely tender,
  Human Deity.—CHO.

4 Jesus, let me love thee,
  Infinitely sweet;
What are the poor odors
  I bring to thy feet?
Yet I love thee, love thee,
  Come into my heart;
And ere long remove me
  To be where thou art.—CHO.
  Rev. E. Paxton Hood.

SONGS OF THE CHRISTIAN LIFE.

OH! THE THOUGHT THAT JESUS LOVES ME.
GEORGE S. WEEKS.

1. Oh! the thought that Je-sus loves me, How my heart with rap-ture swells!
Cho.—Je-sus loves me, Yes, he loves me, Loves me with un-chang-ing love;

Oh! the won-drous, wondrous glad-ness, Which with-in my bos-om dwells.
He will take me, Yes, will take me Soon to his bright home a-bove.

Oh! the thought that Je-sus loves me, This to me is joy un-told,

This to me is rich-est treas-ure, More than ru-bies or than gold.

Copyright, 1875, by George S. Weeks, by per.

173

2 Oh! the thought that Jesus loves me,
  Fills my soul with blissful song,
For his arms of love surround me,
  And enfold me all day long.
Oh! the thought that Jesus loves me,
  With his matchless love and grace,
Takes my heart with longing onward,
  Till I gaze on his fair face.—Cho.

3 Yes, the thought that Jesus loves me,
  Gives me perfect peace and rest,
Like the lov'd disciple's—leaning
  On his Saviour's gentle breast.
Yes, the thought that Jesus loves me
  Fills me with triumphant praise;
Now, Lord Jesus, I can thank thee,
  While my joyful song I raise.—Cho.

E. J. C.

SONGS OF THE CHRISTIAN LIFE.

BREAST THE WAVE, CHRISTIAN. — W. C. FILLEY.

1. Breast the wave, Christian, when it is strongest; Watch for day, Christian, when night is longest; Onward and onward still be thine endeavor, The rest that remaineth, will be forever.

174 *Call to Courage.*

2 Fight the fight, Christian, Jesus is o'er thee;
Run the race, Christian, heaven is before thee;
He who hath promised all, faltereth never,
He who loved so well loveth forever.

3 Lift the eye, Christian, just as it closeth;
Raise the heart, Christian, ere it reposeth;
Thee from the love of Christ, nothing shall sever,
And when thy work is done, praise him forever.

Joseph Stammers.

PERFECT PEACE. — T. E. PERKINS.

1. In heavenly love abiding, No change my heart shall fear; And safe in such confiding,
D.S.—But God is round about me,

SONGS OF THE CHRISTIAN LIFE.

PERFECT PEACE—*Concluded.*

175 *Perfect peace.*

2 Wherever he may guide me,
  No want shall turn me back;
My Shepherd is beside me,
  And nothing can I lack.
His wisdom ever waketh,
  His sight is never dim,
He knows the way he taketh,
  And I will walk with him.

3 Green pastures are before me,
  Which yet I have not seen;
Bright skies will soon be o'er me,
  Where darkest clouds have been.
My hope I cannot measure,
  My path to life is free,
My Saviour has my treasure,
  And he will walk with me.
            Anna L. Waring.

I AM TRUSTING THEE, LORD JESUS.

Permission of Oliver Ditson Co.

176

1 I am trusting thee, Lord Jesus,
    Trusting only thee;
  Trusting thee for full salvation,
    Great and free.

2 I am trusting thee for pardon,
    At thy feet I bow;
  For thy great and tender mercy,
    Trusting now.

3 I am trusting thee, Lord Jesus,
    Never let me fall;
  I am trusting thee forever,
    And for all.
            Miss F. R. Havergal.

SONGS OF THE CHRISTAIN LIFE.

NEARER THE CROSS.   Mrs. J. F. Knapp, by per.

1. "Near-er the cross!" my heart can say, I am com-ing near-er; Near-er the cross from day to day, I am com-ing near-er; Near-er the cross 'where Je-sus died, Near-er the fount-ain's crim-son tide, Near-er my Sav-iour's wound-ed side, I am com-ing near-er, I am com-ing near-er.

177

2 Nearer the Christian's mercy seat,
    I am coming nearer;
Feasting my soul on manna sweet
    I am coming nearer;
Stronger in faith, more clear I see
Jesus who gave himself for me;
Nearer to him I still would be:
    Still I'm coming nearer,
    Still I'm coming nearer.

3 Nearer in prayer my hope aspires
    I am coming nearer:
Deeper the love my soul desires,
    I am coming nearer;
Nearer the end of toil and care,
Nearer the joy I long to share,
Nearer the crown I soon shall wear:
    I am coming nearer,
    I am coming nearer.

F. J. Crosby.

SONGS OF THE CHRISTAIN LIFE.

PENITENCE. 7s, 6s, 8s.   WILLIAM HENRY OAKLEY.

1. Je-sus, let thy pity-ing eye Call back a wan-dering sheep;
False to thee, like Pe-ter, I would fain, like Pe-ter, weep.
Let me be by grace re-stored; On me be all long-suffer-ing shown;
Turn, and look up-on me, Lord, And break my heart of stone.

178 *Humility and contrition.*

2 Saviour, Prince, enthroned above,
  Repentance to impart,
Give me, through thy dying love,
  The humble, contrite heart;
Give what I have long implored,
  A portion of thy grief unknown;
Turn, and look upon me, Lord,
  And break my heart of stone.

3 See me, Saviour, from above,
  Nor suffer me to die;
Life, and happiness, and love
  Drop from thy gracious eye:

Speak the reconciling word,
  And let thy mercy melt me down;
Turn, and look upon me, Lord,
  And break my heart of stone.

4 Look, as when thy languid eye
  Was closed that we might live;
"Father," at the point to die
  My Saviour prayed, "forgive!"
Surely, with that dying word, [done!"
He turns, and looks, and cries, "'Tis
O my bleeding, loving Lord,
  Thou breakest my heart of stone!
          Charles Wesley.

SONGS OF THE CHRISTIAN LIFE.

BRINGING IN THE SHEAVES.

George A. Minor, by per.

SONGS OF THE CHRISTIAN LIFE.

BRINGING IN THE SHEAVES.—*Concluded.*

179

2 Sowing in the sunshine, sowing in the shadows, [ing breeze;
Fearing neither clouds nor winter's chill-
By and by the harvest, and the labor ended, [sheaves.—Cho.
We shall come, rejoicing, bringing in the

3 Going forth with weeping, sowing for the Master, [grieves;
Though the loss sustained our spirit often
When our weeping's over he will bid us welcome, [sheaves.—Cho
We shall come, rejoicing, bringing in the
Knowles Shaw.

NOEL. C. M.   LOWELL MASON.

1. My God, the spring of all my joys, The life of my delights,
The glory of my brightest days, And comfort of my nights!

180 *Triumphant joy.*

2 In darkest shades, if thou appear,
My dawning is begun;
Thou art my soul's bright morning star,
And thou my rising sun.

3 The opening heavens around me shine,
With beams of sacred bliss,
If Jesus shows his mercy mine,
And whispers I am his.

4 My soul would leave this heavy clay
At that transporting word,
Run up with joy the shining way,
To see and praise my Lord.

5 Fearless of hell and ghastly death,
I'd break through every foe;
The wings of love and arms of faith
Would bear me conqueror through.
Isaac Watts.

HEAR US, HOLY JESUS.   Arr. by SULLIVAN.

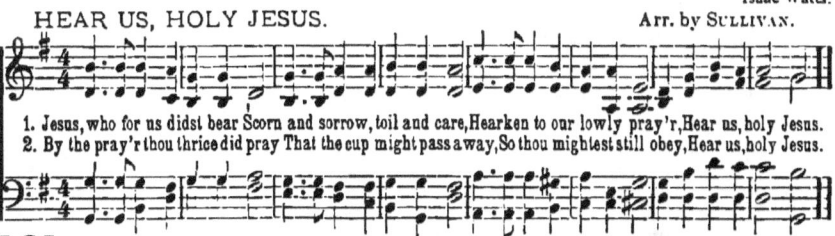

1. Jesus, who for us didst bear Scorn and sorrow, toil and care, Hearken to our lowly pray'r, Hear us, holy Jesus.
2. By the pray'r thou thrice did pray That the cup might pass away, So thou mightest still obey, Hear us, holy Jesus.

181

3 By the cross which thou didst bear,
By the cup they bade thee share,
Mingled gall and vinegar,
Hear us, holy Jesus.

4 When temptation sore is rife,
When we faint amidst the strife,
Thou, whose death has been our life,
Save us, holy Jesus.

SONGS OF THE CHURCH.

SEND THE LIGHT.

CHAS. H. GABRIEL.

The first 8 measures, (or Bass Solo,) may be omitted.

Copyright, 1890, by Chas. H. Gabriel.

SEND THE LIGHT.--*Concluded.*

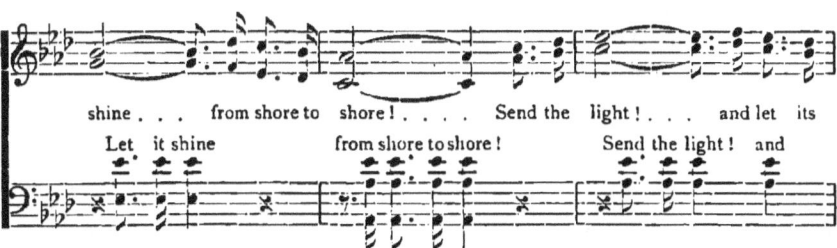

182

2 We have heard the Macedonian call to-day,
"Send the light, send the light!"
And a golden offering at the cross we lay,
Send the light, send the light!—Cho.

3 Let us pray that grace may everywhere abound,
Send the light, send the light!
And a Christ-like spirit everywhere be found,
Send the light, send the light!—Cho.

4 Let us not grow weary in the work of love,
Send the light, send the light!
Let us gather jewels for a crown above,
Send the light, send the light.—Cho.

C. H. G.

SONGS OF THE CHURCH.

183

1 Christian, lo! the fields are whit'ning
  For the harvest of the Lord;
Be not idle, onward ever,
  Ye shall reap a rich reward.—Cho.

2 Onward, Christians, still press onward,
  Singing sweetly as we go;
Strong in faith, we soon shall triumph,
  Tho' opposed by many a foe.—Cho.

3 Christians, lo! the dawn is breaking
  Of a clearer brighter day;
Yield not to the clouds of sorrow,
  Ever onward press your way.—Cho.

4 Girded with the gospel armor,
  Join the war, to battle go;
Armed with faith, with Christ as leader
  Ye shall conquer every foe.—Cho.

R. G. S.

SONGS OF THE CHURCH.

THE BATTLE HYMN OF MISSIONS. JOHN WHITAKER.

184
2 We wait thy triumph, Saviour King;
Long ages have prepared thy way;
Now all abroad thy banner fling,
Set time's great battle in array.

3 Thy hosts are mustered to the field;
"The Cross! the Cross!" the battle call,
The old grim tow'rs of darkness yield
And soon shall totter to their fall.

4 On mountain tops the watchfires glow,
Where scatter'd wide the watchmen stand
Voice echoes voice, and onward flow
The joyous shouts from land to land. ·

5 O fill the Church with faith and pow'r,
Bid her long night of weeping cease;
To groaning nations haste the hour
Of life and freedom, light and peace.
Ray Palmer.

MIGDOL. L. M LOWELL MASON.

185 *That glorious anthem.*
2 Let thrones, and powers, and kingdoms be
Obedient, mighty God, to thee;
And over land, and stream, and main,
Now wave the scepter of thy reign.

3 Oh let that glorious anthem swell ·
Let host to host the triumph tell,
Till not one rebel heart remains,
But over all the Saviour reigns. Mrs. Voke.

SONGS OF THE CHURCH.

I AM THE WAY. CHAS. H. GABRIEL.

Copyright in Scripture Songs. Used by per.

SONGS OF THE CHURCH.

I AM THE WAY.—*Concluded.*

186

1 In from the highways,
In from the by-ways,
Gather souls in Jesus name;
Publish the story,
Herald his glory,
Unto the world his message proclaim.

2 Go to the erring,
Kindly and cheering,
Point them to the crucified;
Rescue the prayerless,
Plead with the careless,
Till they in Jesus safely abide

3 Go, then, believing,
Blessing receiving,
You shall reap reward above;
Jesus is calling,—
Darkness is falling,
On with the blessed labor of love.

Chas. H. Gabriel.

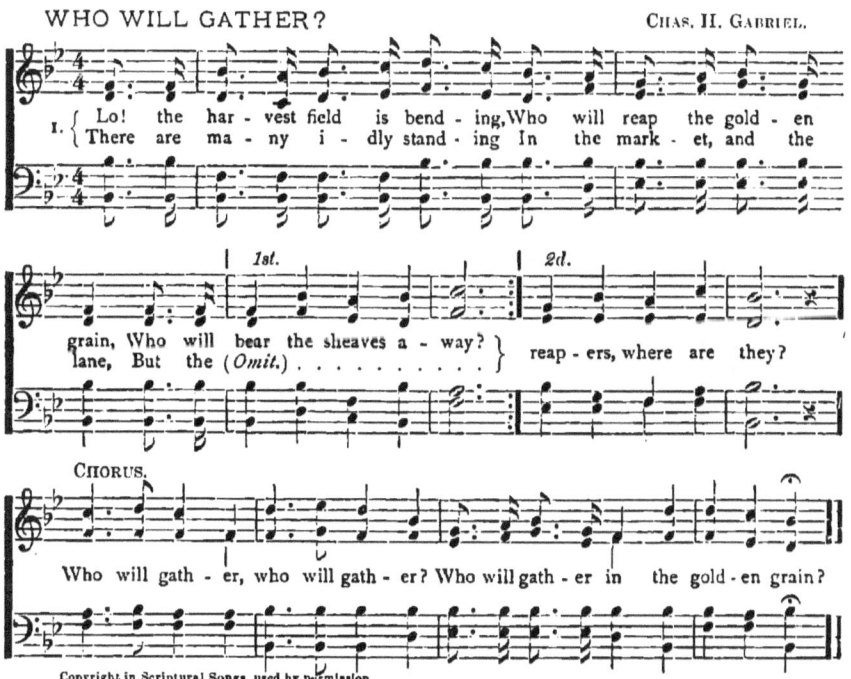

WHO WILL GATHER?   CHAS. H. GABRIEL.

1. Lo! the har-vest field is bend-ing, Who will reap the gold-en grain, Who will bear the sheaves a-way?
There are ma-ny i-dly stand-ing In the mark-et, and the lane, But the (*Omit.*) . . . . reap-ers, where are they?

CHORUS.
Who will gath-er, who will gath-er? Who will gath-er in the gold-en grain?

Copyright in Scriptural Songs, used by permission.

187

2 See the many that are waiting,
'Round about the golden field,
All in idleness to-day;
They have themes, they have suggestions,
For the labor and the yield,
But the reapers, where are they?

3 Hasten, brother, to the harvest,
To the harvest of the Lord!
Gather sheaves from near and far,
So that when the Master calleth,
This shall be the welcome word;—
"Blessed reapers, here they are!"

Chas. H. Gabriel.

SONGS OF THE CHURCH.

IS YOUR LIGHT SHINING? R. G. Staples.

1. Is your light shining brightly, my brother? From sin, and from danger, and
Does it cast a broad gleam o'er the wave?

sorrow Some poor shipwreck'd soul it may save. Let it shine, let it shine, O'er the waves of the
Let it shine, let it shine,

dark, rolling sea; Let it shine, let it shine, So the nations its glory may see.
let it shine, let it shine,

By permission.

188

2 Let it shine with a light bright and cheery,
Let it shine with a light broad and glad;
It may speak peace and hope to the weary,
It may bring joy and trust to the sad.

3 Let your light shine so brightly, my brother,
That others may take note of you,

And glorify Jesus in heaven,
By seeing the good that you do.

4 Let it shine in the homes of the fallen,
And cast a glad radiance within;
Christ pardoned the weak and the sinful,
And died to save them from sin.

Eliza M. Sherman.

WATCHMAN. 7. D. Lowell Mason.

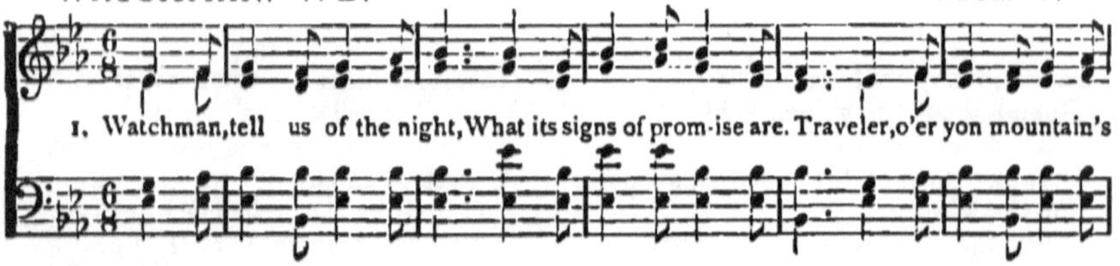

1. Watchman, tell us of the night, What its signs of promise are. Traveler, o'er yon mountain's

SONGS OF THE CHURCH.

WATCHMAN.—*Concluded.*

...height See that glo-ry-beaming star! Watchman, does its beauteous ray Aught of hope or joy fore-tell? Traveler, yes; it brings the day, Promised day of Is-ra-el.

189 *The watchman's report.*

2 Watchman, tell us of the night;
  Higher yet that star ascends.
Traveler, blessedness and light,
  Peace and truth, its course portends!
Watchman, will its beams alone
  Gild the spot that gave them birth?
Traveler, ages are its own,
  See, it bursts o'er all the earth!

3 Watchman, tell us of the night,
  For the morning seems to dawn.
Traveler, darkness takes its flight;
  Doubt and terror are withdrawn.
Watchman, let thy wandering cease;
  Hie thee to thy quiet home!
Traveler, lo! the Prince of peace,
  Lo! the Son of God is come!

  Sir John Bowring.

MISSION SONG. 8s, 7s. D.   P. P. Van Arsdale.

1. Hark! the voice of Jesus calling, Who will go and work to-day? Fields are white, the harvest waiting,
   D.S.—Who will answer, gladly saying,
   Who will bear the sheaves away? Loud and long the Master calleth, Rich reward he of-fers free;
   "Here am I, O Lord, send me."

190 *The laborers are few.*

2 If you cannot cross the ocean
   And the heathen lands explore,
 You can find the heathen nearer,
   You can help them at your door;
 If you cannot speak like angels,
   If you cannot preach like Paul,
 You can tell the love of Jesus,
   You can say he died for all.

3 While the souls of men are dying,
   And the Master calls for you,
 Let none hear you idly saying,
   "There is nothing I can do!"
 Gladly take the task he gives you,
   Let his work your pleasure be;
 Answer quickly when he calleth,
   "Here am I, O Lord, send me."

  D. March.

SONGS OF THE CHURCH.

LEARNING OF JESUS. J. H. F.

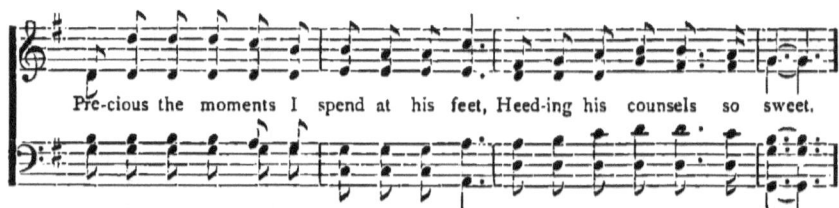

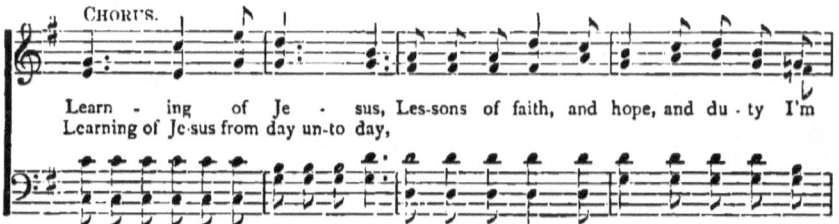

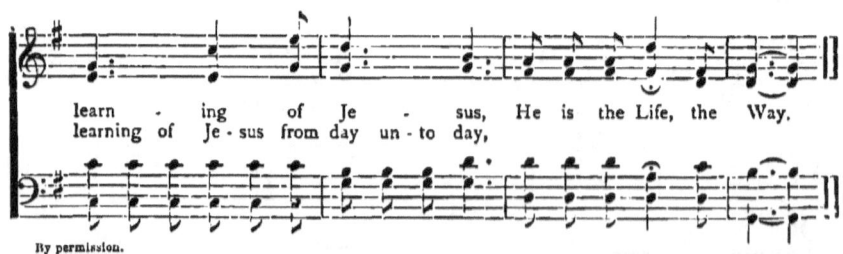

By permission.

191

2 Learning of Jesus, the teacher divine,
Making his precepts and promises mine;
Nothing of all that the world can afford,
Charms me like words from my Lord.

3 Learning of Jesus, the Life and the Way,
His are the words that shall never decay;
Following faithfully, where he says come,
Leads me to heaven and home.

J. H. F.

YOUNG PEOPLE'S SOCIETIES.

GO, LABOR ON.

Robert L. Fletcher.

Copyright, 1891, by Robert L. Fletcher.

192

2 Men die in darkness at your side,
  Without a hope to cheer the tomb;
  Take up the torch and wave it wide—
    The torch that lights time's thickest
      gloom.—Cho.

3 Toil on,—faint not; keep watch and
  Be wise the erring soul to win; [pray!

Go forth into the world's highway;
  Compel the wand'rer to come in.—Cho.

4 Toil on, and in thy toil rejoice;
  For toil comes rest, for exile home;
  Soon shalt thou hear the Bridegroom's
    voice, [Cho.
  The midnight peal: "Behold I come!"
                              Horatius Bonar, arr.

YOUNG PEOPLE'S SOCIETIES.

LOOK UP, LOOK UP TO JESUS.
JOHN HYATT BREWER.

Copyright, 1891, by Hunt & Eaton.

193 *Look Up, Lift Up.*

2 Lift up, lift up to Jesus,
  Each other's helpers be,
His presence shall go with us,
  And give us victory;
Let acts of love and mercy
  Employ our every hour;
Look up, look up to Jesus,
  Who saves us by his power.

3 Look up, look up to Jesus,
  And in his footsteps tread,
Pursue the bright example,
  By his great Spirit led;
Lift up, lift up the fallen,
  And gather in the youth,
By Christ our Lord forgiven,
  Rejoicing in the truth.
    Rev. D. A. Perrin.

YOUNG PEOPLE'S SOCIETIES.

EARNEST WORK FOR JESUS. John Hyatt Brewer.

1. More of earnest work for Jesus, As the passing moments fly;
More of toiling in his vineyard As the sun mounts up the sky;
More of patient, cheerful labour Wrought in faith, and hope, and love;
More of constant, tireless watching, Till we rest with him above.

Copyright, 1891, by Hunt & Eaton.

194

2 More of loving work for Jesus,
  Let us share it day by day:
More of seeking for his glory,
  Ere the daylight fades away,
Ere the dark and chilling midnight
  With its cold and cheerless gloom,
Settling down upon the landscape,
  Points us onward to the tomb.

3 More and better work for Jesus,
  As the months and years go by;
More of trustful, hopeful waiting,
  As the end of life draws nigh;
More and more his word believing,
  Resting in its truth divine,
Till, at last, the crown receiving,
  We shall in his kingdom shine.

W. Bennett.

YOUNG PEOPLE'S SOCIETIES.

PLEDGE HYMN.   WALTER R. JOHNSTON.

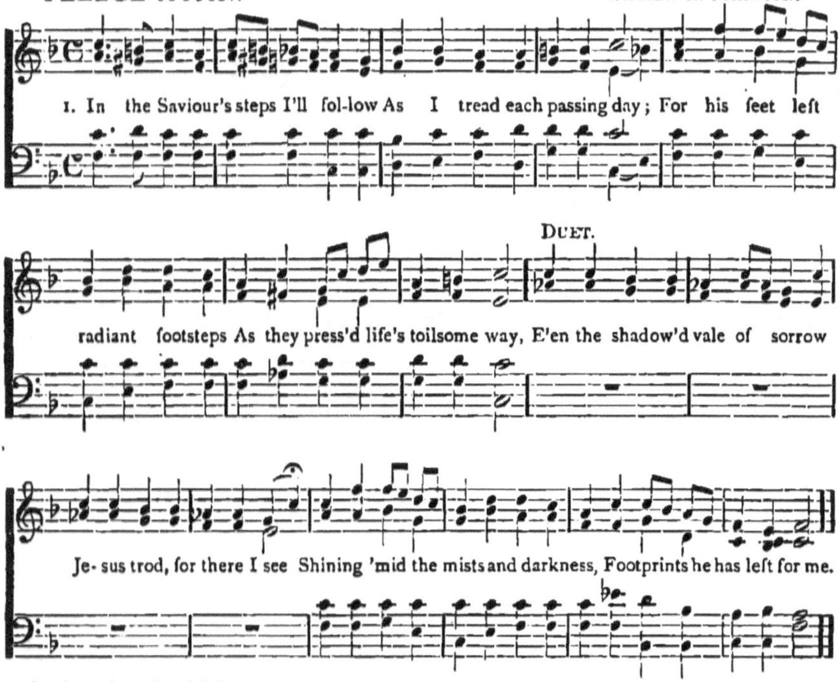

1. In the Saviour's steps I'll fol-low As I tread each passing day; For his feet left radiant footsteps As they press'd life's toilsome way, E'en the shadow'd vale of sorrow Je-sus trod, for there I see Shining 'mid the mists and darkness, Footprints he has left for me.

Copyright, 1891, by Hunt & Eaton.

195

2 Jesus stooped to lift the fallen;
  Left his crown, forsook his throne;
And became for man a servant,
  Wandered weary, scorned, alone.
Saviour, I will seek a lost one,
  I a staff of strength will be
To some pilgrim faint and trembling
  Blindly groping after thee.

3 On the lonely mountain kneeling,
  By the shore of Galilee,
While the starlight fell in beauty,
  Jesus prayed beside the sea.
Father I will seek thy presence,
  That this human heart of mine
May with thee in sweet communion
  Grow in likeness unto thine.
                        E. Craft Cobern.

"DO IT NOW."   Rev. Z. W. FAGAN.

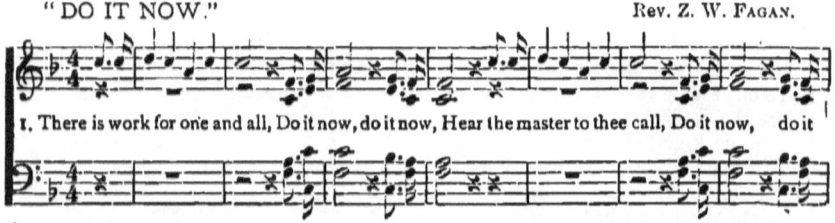

1. There is work for one and all, Do it now, do it now, Hear the master to thee call, Do it now, do it

YOUNG PEOPLE'S SOCIETIES.

"DO IT NOW."—*Concluded.*

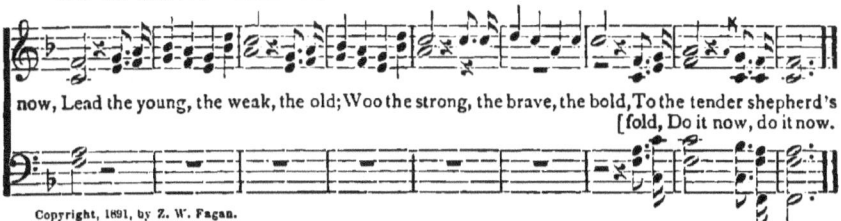

now, Lead the young, the weak, the old; Woo the strong, the brave, the bold, To the tender shepherd's [fold, Do it now, do it now.

Copyright, 1891, by Z. W. Fagan.

196

2 Can you help an erring one?
　Do it now, do it now,
Stay not for "to-morrow's sun,"
　Do it now, do it now.
Bid them leave the path of sin,
And a better life begin;
If some wanderer you can win—
　Do it now, do it now,

3 If for Jesus you can speak,
　Do it now, do it now,
Though your tones are low and weak,
　Do it now, do it now.
Take the tempted by the hand,
Point them to the better land,
That awaits beyond the strand—
　Do it now, do it now.
　　　　　　　　　　　Unknown.

DARWALL. H. M.　　　　　　　　　　　Rev. JOHN DARWALL.

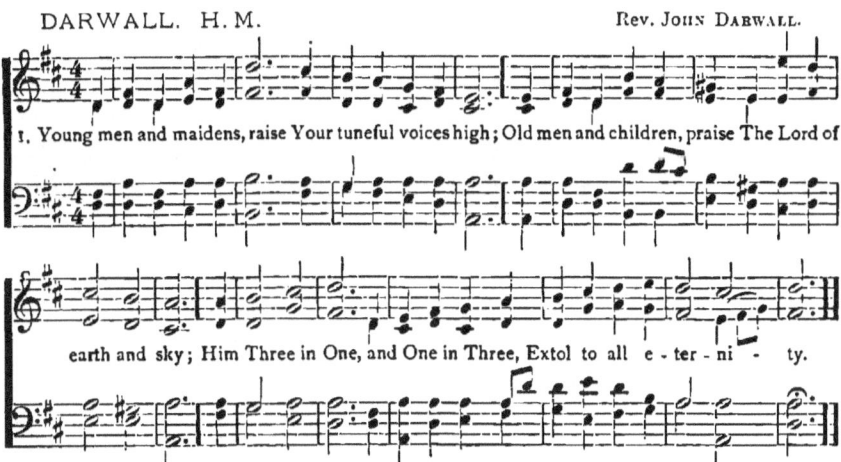

1. Young men and maidens, raise Your tuneful voices high; Old men and children, praise The Lord of earth and sky; Him Three in One, and One in Three, Extol to all e-ter-ni-ty.

197

2 The universal King
　Let all the world proclaim;
Let every creature sing
　His attributes and name:
Him Three in One, and One in Three,
　Extol to all eternity.

3 In his great name alone
　All excellences meet,
Who sits upon the throne,

　And shall forever sit;
Him Three in One, and One in Three,
　Extol to all eternity.

4 Glory to God belongs;
　Glory to God be given,
Above the noblest songs
　Of all in earth and heaven;
Him Three in One, and One in Three,
　Extol to all eternity.
　　　　　　　　　　　Charles Wesley.

YOUNG PEOPLE'S SOCIETIES.
DO SOMETHING TO-DAY.
WM. J. KIRKPATRICK.

1. You're longing to work for the Master, Yet waiting for something to do; You fancy the future is hold-ing Some wonderful mission for you; But while you are waiting the moments Are rap-id-ly pass-ing a-way; O brother, awake from your dreaming, Do something for Jesus to-day.

CHORUS.
Do something, do something, Do something for Jesus to-day;
Do something, do something,
O brother, the moments are pass-ing, Do something for Je-sus to-day.

Copyright, 1888, by Wm. J. Kirkpatrick.

YOUNG PEOPLE'S SOCIETIES.

DO SOMETHING TO-DAY.—*Concluded.*

198

2 Go rescue that wandering brother
Who sinks 'neath his burden of woe,
A single kind action may save him,
If love and compassion you show;
Don't shrink from the vilest about you,
If you can but lead them from sin;
For this is the grandest of missions,—
Lost souls for the Master to win.—Cho.

3 Go sing happy songs of rejoicing
With those who no sorrows have known;
Go weep with the heart-broken mourner,
Go comfort the sad and the lone;

From pitfalls and snares of the tempter
Go rescue the thoughtless and wild:
Go win from pale lips a "God bless you,"
Go brighten the life of a child.—Cho.

4 O never, my brother, stand waiting,
Be willing to do what you can;
The humblest service is needed,
To fill out the Father's great plan;
Be earning your stars of rejoicing
While earth-life is passing away;
Win some one to meet you in glory,—
Do something for Jesus to-day.—Cho.

Lanta Wilson Smith.

WE COME THY PRAISE TO SING. — Walter R. Johnston.

1. We come thy praise to sing; .... We crown thee, glo-rious King, Our sun and shield! Help us to love the light, Help us to do the right, Teach thou our hands to fight, ... And nev-er, nev-er yield.

Copyright, 1891, by Hunt & Eaton.

199

2 When sin our hearts assails,
When faith or courage fails,
Take thou our part;
Bid faith and hope return,
Let love intensely burn,
So that we ever learn
How strong, how strong thou art!

3 O Jesus, ever blest,
Give us thy joy, thy rest,
And keep thine own;
Save us from self and sin,
Make us all pure within,
Then take thy conquerors in
To share, to share thy throne.

Henry Burton, ab.

YOUNG PEOPLE'S SOCIETIES.

THERE'S WORK FOR US ALL.   Chas. H. Gabriel.

Copyright in Scriptural Songs, used by permission.

200

1 There's work for us all in the labor of love,
  Let no one be idle to-day;
  Go gather the gems for the Master above,
  Go, willingly labor and pray.—Cho.

2 There's work for us all wheresoever we be,
  At labor, at home, or abroad;
  Then let us go forth, and we surely shall see
  A bountiful harvest for God.—Cho.

3 There's work for us all! let us go with a prayer,
  That we may find something to do;
  Oh, take up the cross, it is easy to bear;
  Go forth, for the lab'rers are few.—Cho.

C. H. G.

YOUNG PEOPLE'S SOCIETIES.

I WANT TO BE A WORKER.　　　　　　　　　　I. BALTZELL.

201

2 I want to be a worker every day,
I want to lead the erring in the way
That leads to heaven above, where all is peace and love,
In the kingdom of the Lord.—CHO.

3 I want to be a worker strong and brave,
I want to trust in Jesus' power to save ;
All who will truly come, shall find a happy home
In the kingdom of the Lord.—CHO.

4 I want to be a worker ; help me, Lord,
To lead the lost and erring to thy word
That points to joys on high, where pleasures never die,
In the kingdom of the Lord.—CHO.

Isaiah Baltzell.

202. HEAVEN OUR HERITAGE.

Miss Elizabeth Jarrett.   G. Mangold.

1. I watched the ships that come and go Upon the restless sea, And as they hur-ried to and fro, They sent a word to me; A word—from o'er the sea, The winds bore un-to me. "We sail," men say, "up-on the deep, But lo! our masts are
2. I heard the message and I said: "O toiling soul, be wise; Plow on the earth, and dig and sow, But har-vest in the skies; Plant here, but gar-ner there, Thy har-vest in the skies. "Use well the earth—to him that hath Shall all things else be

Copyright, 1891, by Hunt & Eaton.

YOUNG PEOPLE'S SOCIETIES.

HEAVEN OUR HERITAGE.—Concluded.

YOUNG PEOPLE'S SOCIETIES.

O, WE ARE VOLUNTEERS.
GEO. F. ROOT.

1. O, we are vol-un-teers in the ar-my of the Lord, Forming in-to line at our Cap-tain's word; We are un-der marching or-ders to take the bat-tle-field, And we'll ne'er give o'er the fight till the foe shall yield.

CHORUS.
Come and join the army, the army of the Lord, Jesus is our Captain, we ral-ly at his word; Sharp will be the conflict with the pow'rs of sin, But with such a Leader, we we are sure to win.

203

2 The glory of our flag is the emblem of the dove, [love;
Gleaming are our swords from the forge of love;
We go forth, but not to battle for earthly honors vain, [to gain.
'Tis a bright immortal crown that we seek

3 Oh, glorious is the struggle in which we draw the sword,
Glorious is the kingdom of Christ, our Lord;
It shall spread from sea to sea, it shall reach from shore to shore,
And his people shall be blessed forevermore.

From "Silver Chime."

YOUNG PEOPLE'S SOCIETIES.

FORWARD BE OUR WATCHWORD.

Francis Joseph Haydn.

1. Forward! be our watchword, Steps and voices join'd; Seek the things before us, Not a look behind: Burns the fiery pillar At our army's head; Who shall dream of shrinking, By our Captain led? Forward thro' the desert, Thro' the toil and fight; Jordan flows before us, Zion beams with light!

204 *Forward into light.*

2 Forward! flock of Jesus,
  Salt of all the earth,
Till each yearning purpose
  Spring to glorious birth:
Sick, they ask for healing;
  Blind, they grope for day;
Pour upon the nations
  Wisdom's loving ray.
Forward, out of error,
  Leave behind the night;
Forward through the darkness,
  Forward into light!

3 Glories upon glories
  Hath our God prepared,
By the souls that love him
  One day to be shared:
Eye hath not beheld them,
  Ear hath never heard;

Nor of these hath uttered
  Thought or speech a word.
Forward, marching eastward
  Where the heaven is bright,
Till the veil be lifted,
  Till our faith be sight!

4 Far o'er yon horizon
  Rise the city towers,
Where our God abideth;
  That fair home is ours:
Flash the streets with jasper,
  Shine the gates with gold;
Flows the gladdening river
  Shedding joys untold;
Thither, onward thither,
  In the Spirit's might:
Pilgrims to your country,
  Forward into light!

Henry Alford.

YOUNG PEOPLE'S SOCIETIES.

FORTH TO THE FIGHT.
A. B. Gould.

Copyright, 1891, by Hunt & Eaton. Words by permission of Rev. C. L. Hutchins. From S. S. Hymnal.

205

2 Fear not the din of battle,
　Follow where he has trod;
Perfecting strength in weakness—
　Jesus, Incarnate God.—Ref.

3 Arm ye against the battle,
　Watch ye, and fast and pray;
Peace shall succeed the warfare,
　Night shall be changed to day.—Ref.

4 Fight, for the Lord is o'er you,
　Fight, for he bids you fight;
There, when the fray is thickest,
　Close with the hosts of night.—Ref.

W. H. Kirby.

YOUNG PEOPLE'S SOCIETIES.

GO FORWARD CHRISTIAN SOLDIER.

H. P. Danks.

1. Go for-ward, Christian sol-dier! Be-neath his ban-ner true: The Lord himself, thy Lead-er, Shall all thy foes sub-due; His love fore-tells thy tri-als; He knows thine hour-ly need; He can with bread of heav-en, Thy faint-ing spir-it feed.

Copyright, 1891, by H. P. Danks.

206

2 Go forward, Christian soldier!
Fear not the secret foe;
Far more o'er thee are watching
Than human eyes can know:
Trust only Christ, thy Captain;
Cease not to watch and pray;
Heed not the treach'rous voices
That lure thy soul astray.

3 Go forward, Christian soldier!
Nor dream of peaceful rest,
Till Satan's host is vanquished
And heav'n is all possess'd;

Till Christ himself shall call thee
To lay thine armor by,
And wear in endless glory
The crown of victory.

4 Go forward, Christian soldier!
Fear not the gath'ring night:
The Lord has been thy shelter;
The Lord will be thy light;
When morn his face revealeth,
Thy dangers all are past;
Oh, pray that faith and virtue
May keep you to the last!

SONGS OF HEAVEN.

THE WATER OF LIFE.
S. V. R. Ford.

1. The water of life, a clear crystal river, A fountain exhaustless and free; The gift of God's love, a bounding forever, With blessings for you and for me.

REFRAIN.
Pure water of life, blest water of life, From God's great white throne ever flowing; Pure water of life, blest water of life, The joy of salvation bestowing.

Copyright, 1891, by Hunt & Eaton.

207

2 This river makes glad the city up yonder,
   The saints on its borders recline;
   I dwell on the scene with rapture, and wonder
   If ever such bliss will be mine.—Ref.

3 The Saviour extends a glad invitation,
   Give ear to the soul-stirring theme—
   "Come, all ye that thirst, partake of salvation!
   O drink of this life-giving stream!"—Ref.

4 O river of life! O fountain of blessing!
   What joy to the world thou hast given!
   For all such as thirst flow on without ceasing,
   Till earth shall be sinless as heaven!—Ref.

S. V. R. F.

HOME TO-NIGHT.

S. V. R. Ford.

1. O home to-night, yes home to-night, Thro' the pearly gate And the open door,
Some happy feet, on the golden street, Are entering now to go out no more.

FULL-CHORUS.
O home to-night, yes home to-night, Thro' the pearly gate and the open door,
O home to-night, yes home to-night, O home to-night, yes home to-night.
Some happy feet, on the golden street, Are entering now to go out no more.

Copyright, 1891, by Hunt & Eaton.

208

2 For the work is done and the rest begun,
And the training time is forever past;
And the home of rest, in the mansions blest,
Is safely and joyously reached at last.—Cho.

3 O the love and light in that home to-night,
O the songs of bliss and the harps of gold;
O the glory shed on the new-crowned head,
O the telling of love that can ne'er be told.—Cho.

4 O the joy that waits at the shining gates
For the dearly loved far away yet near,
When we all shall meet at his blessed feet,
In the light and love of his home so dear.—Cho

SONGS OF HEAVEN.

ONE SWEETLY SOLEMN THOUGHT. Philip Phillips.

By permission.

209

2 Nearer my Father's house,
   Where many mansions be;
Nearer the great white throne to-day,
Nearer the crystal sea.—Cho.

3 Nearer the bound of life,
   Where burdens are laid down;

Nearer to leave the cross to-day,
And nearer to the crown.—Cho.

4 Be near me when my feet
   Are slipping o'er the brink,
For I am nearer home to-day,
Perhaps, than now I think.—Cho.

Phœbe Carey.

OUT ON AN OCEAN ALL BOUNDLESS WE RIDE. C. S. Harrington.

OUT ON AN OCEAN ALL BOUNDLESS, ETC.—*Concluded.*

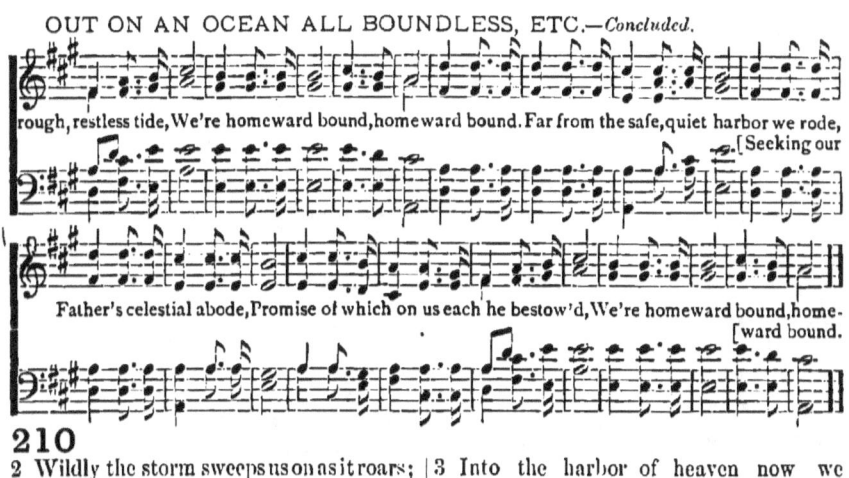

rough, restless tide, We're homeward bound, homeward bound. Far from the safe, quiet harbor we rode, [Seeking our Father's celestial abode, Promise of which on us each he bestow'd, We're homeward bound, homeward bound.

210

2 Wildly the storm sweeps us on as it roars;
　We're homeward bound, homeward bound;
Look! yonder lie the bright heavenly shores;
　We're homeward bound, homeward bound.
Steady! O pilot! stand firm at the wheel,
Steady! we soon shall out-weather the gale; [sail;
Oh! how we fly 'neath the loud creaking
　We're homeward bound, homeward bound.

3 Into the harbor of heaven now we glide,
　We're home at last, home at last;
Softly we drift on its bright silver tide,
　We're home at last, home at last.
Glory to God! all our dangers are o'er;
Safely we stand on the radiant shore,
Glory to God! we will shout evermore,
　We're home at last, home at last.

Author unknown.

JERUSALEM. C. M.

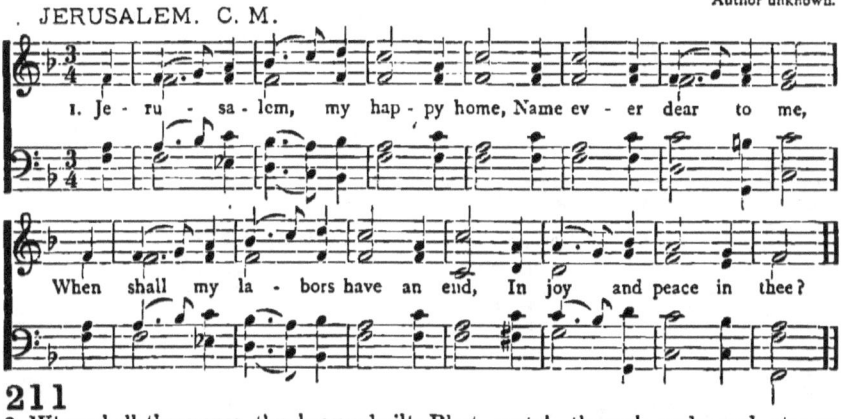

1. Je - ru - sa - lem, my hap - py home, Name ev - er dear to me, When shall my la - bors have an end, In joy and peace in thee?

211

2 When shall these eyes thy heaven-built
　And pearly gates behold? [walls,
Thy bulwarks with salvation strong,
　And streets of shining gold?
3 There happier bow'rs than Eden's bloom,
　Nor sin nor sorrow know:

Blest seats! through rude and stormy
I onward press to you. [scenes
4 Jerusalem, my happy home,
　My soul still pants for thee;
Then shall my labors have an end,
　When I thy joys shall see.

From Francis Baker, ab. 1628.

SONGS OF HEAVEN.

GOING HOME AT LAST. 7s, 6s.
E. S. Lorenz.

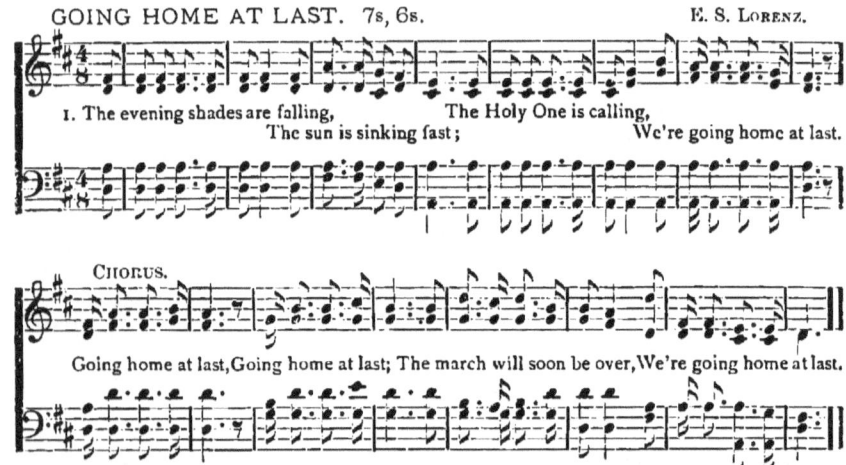

By permission.

212

1 The evening shades are falling,
The sun is sinking fast:
The Holy One is calling,
We're going home at last.—Cho.

2 The road's been long and dreary,
The toils came thick and fast;
In body weak and weary,
We're going home at last.—Cho.

3 We now are nearing heaven,
And soon shall be at rest;
Our crowns will soon be given,
We're going home at last.—Cho.

4 Oh, praise the Lord forever,
Our sorrows are all past;
We'll part no more, no, never;
We are at home at last.—Cho.

Rev. W. Gossett.

FOREVER WITH THE LORD. S. M. D.
I. B. Woodbury.

By permission.

SONGS OF HEAVEN.

FOREVER WITH THE LORD.—*Concluded.*

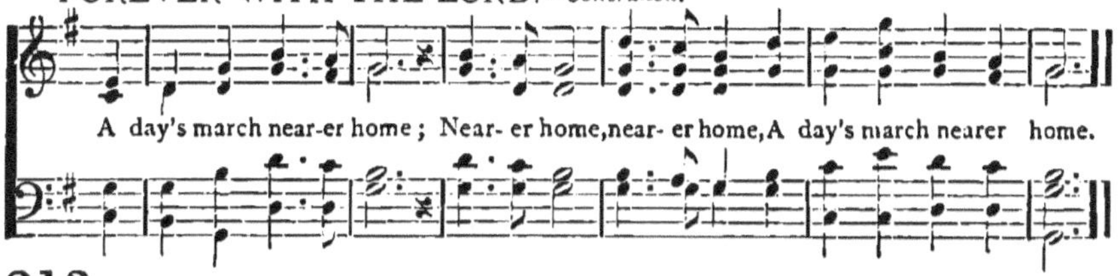

A day's march near-er home; Near- er home, near- er home, A day's march nearer home.

213

2 My Father's house on high,
Home of my soul, how near,
At times, to faith's aspiring eye
Thy golden gates appear.
Ah! then my spirit faints
To reach the land I love;
The bright inheritance of saints—
Jerusalem above;
Home above, home above,
Jerusalem above.

3 Yet doubts still intervene,
And all my comfort flies;
Like Noah's dove, I flit beween
Rough seas and stormy skies.
Anon the clouds depart,
The wind and waters cease,
While sweetly o'er my gladdened heart
Expands the bow of peace:
Bow of peace, bow of peace,
Expands the bow of peace.

James Montgomery.

FULLNESS OF JOY.

S. V. R. Ford.

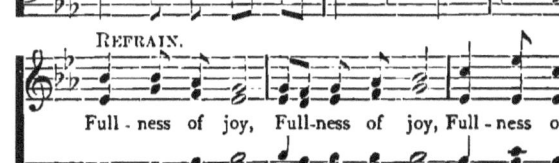

1. Full-ness of joy for-ev-er-more, O sweet and sa-cred word to me;
My will-ing soul would glad-ly soar, That thy great full-ness it might see.

REFRAIN.
Full-ness of joy, Full-ness of joy, Full-ness of joy for-ev-er-more.

Copyright, 1891, by Hunt & Eaton.

214

2 Fullness of sorrow here, O Lord
We have, for we are full of sin;
Speak but the sweet and healing word,
Fullness of peace shall enter in.-REF.

3 Forevermore, e'en this glad hour,
If we his promises believe
Who waiting, standeth at the door,
Fullness of joy we shall receive.-REF.

Lucy B. White.

SONGS OF HEAVEN.

THE SWEET OLDEN STORY. M. S. KERBY.

1. I have read of the sweet olden sto - ry, Of the fair, happy E - den a - bove; Of the beau-ti-ful mansions of glo - ry, In the bright gold-en cit - y of love.

CHORUS.

Oh, the sweet old - en sto - ry Of the fair, hap-py E - den a-bove;
Oh, the sweet old sto - ry dear, Of the fair hap-py E-den a-bove;
Of the beau-ti-ful mansions of glo- ry, In the bright golden city of love.

Copyright, in Scriptural songs, used by permission.

215

2 I have read of the clear sparkling river,
  Bursting out 'neath the great throne of God;
How its sweet waters glide on forever,
  Making glad all the host of the Lord.

3 I have read how the banks of that river,
  By the saints and the angels are trod,
How their glorious anthems forever,
  Swell the praise of our Saviour and Lord.

H. S. Kerby.

SONGS OF HEAVEN.

REJOICE AND BE GLAD. S. V. R. Ford.

1. Rejoice and be glad, ye children of Zion, The Lord hath redeem'd you, Exult in his name; Your foes shall no longer with bondage oppress you, No longer rejoice in your sorrow and shame. Rejoice and be glad, ye children of Zion, Rejoice and be glad in Jesus your King.

Copyright, 1891, by Hunt & Eaton.

216

2 The Lord hath cast up a highway to glory,
 For those he hath ransom'd from bondage to sin;
 The vile and unholy shall never pass o'er it;
 The righteous shall journey with safety therein.—Ref.

3 All sorrow and sighing, all anguish and sadness,
 Shall vanish like darkness at dawn of the day;
 All rapture celestial, all joy and all gladness
 Shall come to the ransom'd who walk in this way.—Ref.

S. V. R. Ford.

SONGS FOR THE LITTLE ONES.

KIND WORDS CAN NEVER DIE.
ABBY HUTCHINSON.

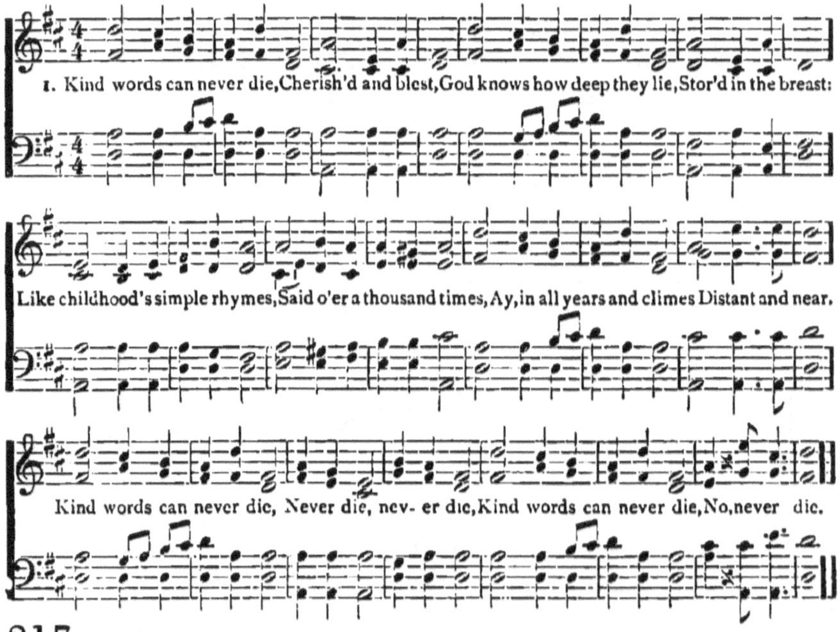

1. Kind words can never die, Cherish'd and blest, God knows how deep they lie, Stor'd in the breast;

Like childhood's simple rhymes, Said o'er a thousand times, Ay, in all years and climes Distant and near.

Kind words can never die, Never die, nev- er die, Kind words can never die, No, never die.

217

2 Sweet thoughts can never die,
 Though, like the flowers,
Their brightest hues may fly
 In wintry hours.
But when the gentle dew
Gives them their charms anew,
With many an added hue
 They bloom again.
Sweet thoughts can never die,
 Never die, never die,
Sweet thoughts can never die,
 No, never die.

3 Our souls can never die,
 Though in the tomb
We may all have to lie,
 Wrapped in its gloom.
What though the flesh decay,
Souls pass in peace away,
Live through eternal day
 With Christ above.
Our souls can never die,
 Never die, never die,
Our souls can never die,
 No, never die.
  Miss A. Hutchinson.

GLORY TO THE FATHER GIVE.
H. P. DANKS.

1. Glo-ry to the Fa-ther give, God in whom we move and live; Children's pray'rs he

SONGS FOR THE LITTLE ONES.

GLORY TO THE FATHER GIVE.—*Concluded.*

Copyright, 1891, by H. P. Danks.

218

2 Glory to the Holy Ghost,
He reclaims the sinner lost;
Children's minds may he inspire,
Touch their tongues with holy fire.

Glory in the highest be
To the blessed Trinity,
For the gospel from above,
For the word that "God is love."
J. Montgomery.

OUR HEAVENLY GUIDE.   S. V. R. FORD.

Copyright, 1891, by Hunt & Eaton.

219

2 Our being and our blessing
  Are from thy bounteous hand;
Our sinfulness confessing,
  We'll serve at thy command.
Accept the gifts we offer;
  Defend us by thy might;
Use all the powers we proffer
  In service of the right.

3 Our lives, enthroning Duty,
  And radiant in its light,
Shall be "a thing of beauty,"
  All jubilant and bright.
Our way shall ne'er be dreary
  With thy dear presence blest;
Our hearts shall ne'er grow weary
  Till toil shall end in rest.

C. H. Payne.

SONGS FOR THE LITTLE ONES.

CHILDREN OF JERUSALEM. ENGLISH MELODY.

220

1 Children of Jerusalem
Sang the praise of Jesus' name;
Children too of modern days,
Join to sing the Saviour's praise.—Cho.

2 We have often heard and read
What the royal psalmist said,
Babes and sucklings' artless lays,
Shall proclaim the Saviour's praise.—Cho.

3 We are taught to love the Lord;
We are taught to read his word;
We are taught the way to heaven:
Praise for all to God be given!—Cho.

4 Parents, teachers, old and young,
All unite to swell the song:
Higher and yet higher rise,
Till hosannas reach the skies.—Cho.

John Henley.

SONGS FOR THE LITTLE ONES.

IF I COME TO JESUS.
W. H. Doane, by per.

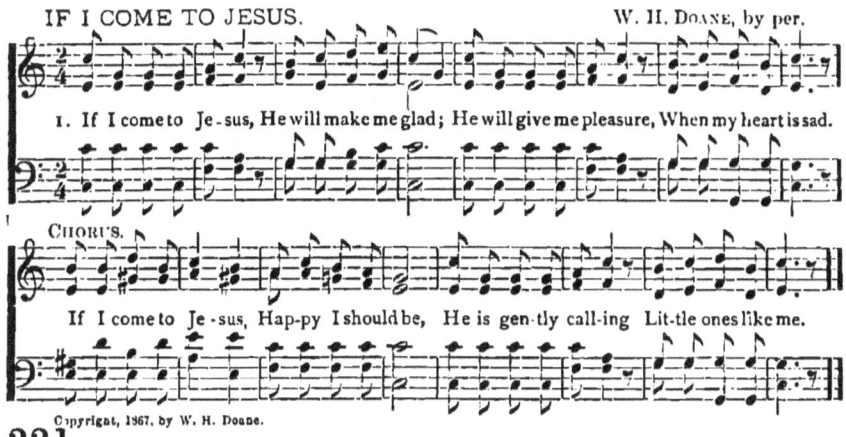

Copyright, 1867, by W. H. Doane.

221

1 If I come to Jesus,
  He will make me glad ;
  He will give me pleasure,
  When my heart is sad.—Cho.

2 If I come to Jesus,
  He will hear my prayer ;
  He will love me dearly,
  He my sins did bear.—Cho.

3 If I come to Jesus,
  He will take my hand ;
  He will kindly lead me
  To a better land.—Cho.

4 There with happy children,
  Robed in snowy white,
  I shall see my Saviour
  In that world so bright.—Cho.

SEE, ISRAEL'S GENTLE SHEPHERD STANDS.
William V. Wallace.

222 *Suffer the little ones to come unto me.*

2 " Permit them to approach," he cries,
  " Nor scorn their humble name ;
  For 'twas to bless such souls as these
  The Lord of angels came."

3 We bring them, Lord, in thankful hands,
  And yield them up to thee ;
  Joyful that we ourselves are thine,
  Thine let our offspring be.

Philip Doddridge.

SONGS FOR THE LITTLE ONES.

223. LORD, TEACH A CHILD TO PRAY.

ARZELIA DUPIGNAC.
Moderato.
WALTER R. JOHNSTON.

1. Lord, teach a child to pray, As I wake at peep of day; Watch o'er me while I play, In my hap-py, childish way. If I am good and kind God will sure be by my side; Help Lord that I may find The nar-row road, not the wide.
2. Re-member Lord and guide, My foot-steps the road I glide; To all who fol-low me, An ex-am-ple let me be. Grow-ing I'd like to be All that God requires of me, My heart from care be free, Then my soul will rest with thee.

Copyright, 1891, by Hunt & Eaton.

SONGS FOR THE LITTLE ONES.

TO-DAY HE IS CALLING.

GEORGE S. WEEKS.

By per. of George S. Weeks, owner of copyright.

224

2 There's rest for the weary, there's hope for the sad,
Strength for the fallen, yes, all may be glad;
There's a home for the friendless, and wealth for the poor,
Jesus stands waiting to open the door.—Cho.

3 Perhaps some have listened, his sweet voice have heard
Echoed in living tones found in his word;
Oh, heed now the calling—why longer delay?
List to his bidding—yes, this very day.—Cho.

G. S. W.

SONGS FOR THE LITTLE ONES.

JESUS, FRIEND OF CHILDREN, HEAR.
George S. Weeks.

1. Thou who once with man didst dwell, Thou whose tendr'st accents fell, When the little ones drew near, Je-sus, friend of children, hear. Now in youth's fair morning hour, Whilst the dew is on the flow'r, Ev-er, Saviour be thou near, Je-sus, friend of children, hear.

Copyright, 1875, by George S. Weeks.

225

2 When by parents, pastors taught,
Check, O Lord, each wand'ring tho't;
Teach us reverence and fear,
Jesus, our petitions hear.
When in after years we roam
Far from teachers, far from home,
Guide us, guard us, Saviour dear,
Jesus, friend of children, hear.

3 If success in life be ours,
All our path be strewn with flowers,
In our happiness be near,
"Light of Light," in mercy hear.

Or if poverty's low cot,
Pain or suffering be our lot,
Thou the drooping heart canst cheer,
Friend of mourners, then be near.

4 If preserved to hoary age,
Keep us in life's latest stage;
When the gate of death is near,
Lighten thou the passage drear.
Then when life's brief course is run,
Thou our hope, our shield, our sun,
Like to thee may we appear,
Jesus, Saviour, hear, O hear.

G. Dew——.

JESUS, TENDER SHEPHERD.
Rev. John B Dykes.

1. Je-sus, ten-der Shepherd, hear me, Bless thy lit-tle lamb to-night;

SONGS FOR THE LITTLE ONES.

JESUS, TENDER SHEPHERD.—*Concluded.*

Through the darkness be thou near me, Keep me safe till morning light. A-men.

226

2 All this day thy hand has led me,
And I thank thee for thy care;
Thou hast clothed me, warmed and fed me,
Listen to my evening prayer.

3 Let my sins be all forgiven,
Bless the friends I love so well;
Take me, when I die, to heaven,
Happy there with thee to dwell.

Mrs. Mary L. Duncan.

LITTLE ONE, COME TO ME. H. R. PALMER.

1. Soft-ly, soft-ly, Christ is call-ing, "Lit-tle one, come to me;"
Hear the sil-v'ry ech-oes fall-ing, Mu-sic sweet the soul en-thrall-ing,
"Come to me, come to me, Lit-tle one, come to me." A-men.

Copyright, 1887, by H. R. Palmer.

227

2 "Come when life's fair morn is brightest,
   Little one, come to me;
Come while thy young heart is lightest,
Come ere thou the Spirit blightest,
   Linger not, linger not,
   Little one, come to me."

3 "They that early seek shall find me,
   Little one come to me;
Let not sinful pleasures blind thee,
Hasten, ere the tempter bind thee,
   Come just now, come just now,
   Little one, come to me."

SONGS FOR THE LITTLE ONES.

FORBID THEM NOT.
H. D. Leslie.

1. There is no sweeter story told, In all the blessed book, Than how the Lord with-in his arms The little children took. We love him for the tender touch, That made the leper whole, And for the wondrous words that heal'd The weary sin-sick soul. And for the wondrous words that heal'd The weary sin-sick soul,

Copyright, 1891, by Hunt & Eaton.

228

2 But closer to his loving self,
  Our human hearts are brought,
When, for the little Children's sake
  Zion's sweetest spell is wrought.
For their young eyes his sorrowing face
  A smile of gladness wore,
‖: A smile that for his little ones,
  It weareth evermore. :‖

3 The voice that silenced priest and scribe
  For them grew low and sweet,
And still for them his gentle lips
  The loving words repeat.
"Forbid them not," O blessed Christ,
  We bring them unto thee,
‖: And pray that on their heads may rest
  The benedicite. :‖

Mary B. Sleight.

SONGS—MISCELLANEOUS.

TEMPERANCE RALLY.
D. S. Hakes.

1. Rally for the cause of temp'rance, Childhood, youth, and age; Let each name now seek an entrance On the temp'rance page. Sign the pledge, abstain from e-vil In thy youth-ful days, Lest thou walk so lone and feeble In the drunkard's ways. Sign the pledge and wear the ribbon, Don the badge of blue; Seek the tempted and the fall-en, God will strengthen you.

Copyright, 1878, by J. E. White.

229

2 Take the water sparkling brightly,
   God hath given free,
If in life so gay and sprightly
   Thou would'st ever be.
Shun the wine ere hearts be broken
   O'er the final fall;
Listen to our warnings, spoken,
   Heed our temp'rance call.—Cho.

3 Let the cheering words be spoken
   To the tempted soul;
Bind the threads of hope now broken
   By the cruel bowl;
Bid him now take courage, moving
   Forward for the right:
God will look with smiles approving,
   Helping by his might.—Cho.

F. E. Belden.

SONGS—MISCELLANEOUS.

230

1 Did you hear the loving word?
  Pass it on, pass it on!
Like the singing of a bird?
  Pass it on, pass it on!
Let its music live and grow,
Let it cheer another's woe;
You have reaped what others sow,
  Pass it on, pass it on!—Cho.

3 Have you found the heavenly light?
  Pass it on, pass it on!
Souls are groping in the night,
  Daylight gone, daylight gone!
Hold your lighted lamp on high,
Be a star in some one's sky,
He may live who else would die,
  Pass it on, pass it on!—Cho.
      Rev. Henry Burton, A. M.

SONGS—MISCELLANEOUS.

MY NATIVE LAND. Wm. J. Kirkpatrick.

1. My native land! my native land! I love thee, O my native land;
Thy valleys and thy noble hills, Thy oceans, lakes, and rippling rills;

CHORUS.
My native land, dear native land! I love thee, O my native land!
My native land, dear native land! I love thee, O my native land!

Copyright, 1889, by Wm. J. Kirkpatrick.

231

2 My native land, home of the free,
I love thy songs of liberty;
Thy brilliant banners, floating high,
Whose starry folds embrace the sky.

3 My native land, in proud delight,
I cherish thee, where right is might,
A land redeemed by patriot blood,
And guarded by the patriot's God.

4 My native land! Religion rules!
The Bible and the common schools!
Here knowledge is a potent rod,
And all are free to worship God.

Rev. E. H. Stokes, D. D.

SONGS—MISCELLANEOUS.

GREETING GLEE. D. S. HAKES.

Copyright, 1880, by J. E. White.

232

2 To grief and care a long adieu,
  To joy alone our hearts are thrall;
  With gladsome song we welcome you,
  For gay and joyous are we all.—Cho.

3 May sweetest flowers deck the way
  Where'er in life our path may be;
  And heaven's brightest, fairest day
  Reign over us eternally.—Cho.

F. E. Belden.

SONGS—MISCELLANEOUS.

HELP THE ERRING.   D. S. HAKES.

1. Help the err-ing, help the wea-ry, Help the doubt-ing, hope-less one;
Though the way be dark and drea-ry, Nev-er leave thy task un-done.

CHORUS.
Help the weak and err-ing broth-er, Raise the fall-en, cheer the sad;
Lend a will-ing hand to help them—Make the poor and need-y glad.

Copyright, 1889, by J. E. White.

233

2 Life is but a field of labor—
Do not strive for self alone;
Live for God and for your neighbor,
And let charity be shown.—Cho.

3 Words of courage ever speaking,
Seek the straying ones to win;
And the lost and wayward seeking,
Bid them leave the paths of sin.–Cho.

4 This should be our high ambition—
Love for God and fellow man;
This our grand and noble mission—
Lending aid to all we can.—Cho.

F. E. Belden.

SONGS—MISCELLANEOUS.

GLADLY WE HAIL THIS FESTAL DAY.

S. V. R. Ford.

1. Gladly we hail . . . . . this festal day, Bringing rest to weary workers in the vineyard of the Lord; Gladly our hearts . . . . their homage pay To our kind and loving Father who will all our toil reward. In joyful strains . . his praise we sing, ... Who came to earth from heav'n afar, And left the pearly gates ajar; Good will and peace . . . toward men to bring, . . . The Christ, the Bright and Morning Star.

Copyright, 1891, by Hunt & Eaton.

SONGS—MISCELLANEOUS.

GLADLY WE HAIL THIS FESTAL DAY.—*Concluded.*

234

2 Hither we come, a happy throng,
Love and loyalty confessing to the reigning Prince of Peace;
Him we adore; to him belong
(Glory, honor, power and blessing, and his kingdom shall increase!—Cho

3 Glory to God, who reigns above,
Father, Son and Holy Spirit, 'throned in peerless majesty!
Shout the refrain that God is love!
Let it echo! echo! echo! over every land and sea!—Cho.

S. V. R. F.

ROUND THE THRONE OF GLORY. L. O. E.

1. Round the throne of glo - ry, Cir - cling cher-u - bim Raise their hal-low'd voic - es In the sa - cred hymn; True their notes are blend - ed, Loud the strains they raise, Thro' the courts e - ter - nal Roll the songs of praise;

235

2 Earth with many voices
Blended with the sea,
Pealing forth the anthem
Of their praise to thee;
Night and day it rises,
Mingling with the song
Which those sacred singers
Endlessly prolong.

3 Where the city steeple
And the village spire
Point each faithful toiler
To his soul's desire,
There in faith we gather,
There our homage pay,
Prayer and praise we offer
On each hallow'd day.

SONGS—MISCELLANEOUS.

MARCHING ON TO ZION.   S. V. R. FORD.

1. Soldiers of Christ, a holy cause defending, Arm'd with the weapons of truth and righteousness;
Faith-ful and true, on his right arm depending, On to the cit-y of God we press.

CHORUS.

Marching, marching, marching on to Zi-on, 'Neath the ban-ner of the King of kings!
Marching, marching, marching on to Zi-on, Heav'n with our an-them of triumph rings!

Copyright, 1891, by Hunt & Eaton.

236

2 Hark! hark! the voice of Christ our Captain, saying, [the word;
"Lo! I am with you!" How cheering is
Valiant we'll be, nor doubt nor fear displaying,
Strong in the might of our risen Lord.

3 Blessed are they who with their Lord and Master [of sin;
Share in the conflict against the hosts
Fighting for him, they cannot know disaster;
Jesus is mighty, and they shall win.
         S. V. R. F.

SONGS—MISCELLANEOUS.

READY FOR LABOR. Wm. F. Sherwin.

Copyright, 1880, by J. E. White.

237

2 Ready to cheer the sad and weak,
Ready the erring soul to seek,
Ready with songs to praise our King,
Ready with all we have to bring.—Cho.

3 Ready to stand for right alone,
Ready to boldly make it known,

Ready to "hold the fort" for aye,
Ready to march at early day.—Cho.

4 Ready as soldiers, firm and true,
Ready our Master's work to do,
Ready to hold our banner high,
Ready to dare and do and die.—Cho.

Eliza H. Morton.

SONGS—MISCELLANEOUS.

'TIS SUMMER TIME. W. A. OGDEN.

1. The gen- tle winds are blow-ing, 'Tis sum-mer time a - gain; The singing brooks are flowing Thro' ev- 'ry glade and glen; Glad summer time re - veal-ing God's treasures rich and rare, While joy ous bells are peal- ing, To banish gloom and care. The birds that sing in leaf- y bow'rs, Are not more blithe than we, As here we meet among the flow'rs, With spirits light and free.

Copyright, 1891, by Robert L. Fletcher.

238

2 The sun is brightly beaming,
   All nature smiles to-day;
The golden light is gleaming
   To cheer the onward way;
In holy contemplation
   We look to God above;
We praise him for salvation,
   And all his wondrous love.—CHO.

3 This day of floral greeting,
   We come a happy throng,
And spend the moments fleeting,
   In mirth and joyous song;
O day of richest treasure!
   O day among the flowers!
We sing in tuneful measure,
   To bless the waking hours.—CHO.

239 *The courts of the Lord.*

3 Happy souls! their praises flow,
Ever in this vale of woe;
Waters in the desert rise,
Manna feeds them from the skies;
On they go from strength to strength,
Till they reach thy throne at length;
At thy feet adoring fall,
Who hast led them safe through all.

4 Lord, be mine this prize to win;
Guide me through a world of sin,
Keep me by thy saving grace,
Give me at thy side a place;
Sun and shield alike thou art;
Guide and guard my erring heart;
Grace and glory flow from thee;
Shower, O shower them, Lord on me.

H. F. Lyte.

SONGS—MISCELLANEOUS.

ALLELUIA! SWEETLY SING.
FREDERIC ALLDRED.

Copyright, 1891, by Hunt & Eaton.

240

1 All is bright and cheerful round us,
  All above is soft and blue!
Every flower is full of gladness,
  Summer hath brought its pleasures too!

2 There are leaves that never wither,
  There are flowers that ne'er decay,
Nothing evil goeth thither,
  Nothing good is kept away.
          J. M. Neale

BOLTON. 7s, 6s. JOHN WALSH.

1. Sing to the Lord of har-vest! Sing songs of love and praise! With joyful hearts and

220

SONGS—MISCELLANEOUS.

BOLTON.—*Concluded.*

voic-es Your hal-le-lu-jahs raise: By him the roll-ing sea-sons In fruit-ful or-der move; Sing to the Lord of har-vest A song of hap-py love.

241 *Praise to the Lord of harvest.*

2 By him the clouds drop fatness,
　The deserts bloom and spring,
　The hills leap up in gladness,
　The valleys laugh and sing:
　He filleth with his fullness
　All things with large increase;
　He crowns the year with goodness,
　With plenty, and with peace.

3 Heap on his sacred altar
　The gifts his goodness gave,
　The golden sheaves of harvest,
　The souls he died to save:

Your hearts lay down before him
　When at his feet ye fall,
And with your lives adore him
　Who gave his life for all.

4 To God, the gracious Father,
　Who made us "very good,"
To Christ, who, when we wandered
　Restored us with his blood,
And to the Holy Spirit,
　Who doth upon us pour
His blessed dews and sunshine,
　Be praise for evermore!

　　　　　　　　John S. B. Monsell.

THE LORD'S PRAYER.
242

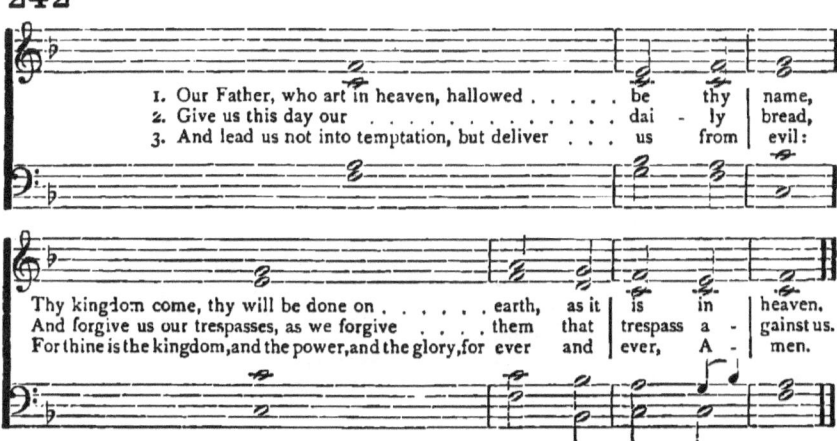

1. Our Father, who art in heaven, hallowed . . . . . be thy name,
2. Give us this day our . . . . dai - ly bread,
3. And lead us not into temptation, but deliver . . . us from evil:

Thy kingdom come, thy will be done on . . . . . earth, as it is in heaven.
And forgive us our trespasses, as we forgive . . . . them that trespass a - gainst us.
For thine is the kingdom, and the power, and the glory, for ever and ever, A - men.

SONGS—MISCELLANEOUS.

ALL THE WAY.   Frank M. Davis.

1. All the way the Saviour leads me, All the way, all the way;
All my needs He doth supply me, All the way, all the way;
And his goodness faileth never; He is mine, yes, mine forever;
From his love I ne'er can sever, All the way, all the way.

By permission.

243

2 All the way the Saviour leads me,
    All the way, all the way;
With the heavenly manna feeds me,
    All the way, all the way.
Though the path be dark and dreary,
And my feet have grown so weary,
Yet he makes life seem so cheery,
    All the way, all the way.

3 All the way the Saviour leads me,
    All the way, all the way;
To the living waters guides me,
    All the way, all the way.
What care I for earthly treasure,
What care I for worldly pleasure?
I have grace beyond the measure,
    All the way, all the way.
                   Frank M. Davis.

SONGS—MISCELLANEOUS.

244. GLORIA PATRI.

Arr. by W. R. Johnston.

Copyright, 1891, by Hunt & Eaton.

SHIRLAND. S. M.

246 *Knowledge of forgiveness.*

1 How can a sinnner know
  His sins on earth forgiven?
  How can my gracious Saviour show
  My name inscribed in heaven?

2 What we have felt and seen
  With confidence we tell;
  And publish to the sons of men
  The signs infallible.

3 We who in Christ believe
  That he for us hath died,
  We all his unknown peace receive,
  And feel his blood applied.

4 Exults our rising soul,
  Disburdened of her load,
  And swells unutterably full
  Of glory and of God.

5 His love, surpassing far
  The love of all beneath,
  We find within our hearts, and dare
  The pointless darts of death.

6 Stronger than death or hell
  The sacred power we prove;
  And conquerors of the world, we dwell
  In heaven, who dwell in love.
  Charles Wesley.

RATHBUN. 8s, 7s.

247 *The desire of nations.*

1 Come, thou long-expected Jesus,
  Born to set thy people free:
  From our fears and sins release us,
  Let us find our rest in thee.

2 Israel's Strength and Consolation,
  Hope of all the earth thou art;
  Dear Desire of every nation,
  Joy of every longing heart.

3 Born thy people to deliver,
  Born a child, and yet a King,
  Born to reign in us forever,
  Now thy gracious kingdom bring.

4 By thine own eternal Spirit,
  Rule in all our hearts alone;
  By thine all-sufficient merit,
  Raise us to thy glorious throne.
  Charles Wesley.

COMMUNION. C. M.

248 *He died for thee.*

1 Behold the Saviour of mankind
  Nailed to the shameful tree;
  How vast the love that him inclined
  To bleed and die for thee!

2 Hark! how he groans, while nature shakes,
  And earth's strong pillars bend;
  The temple's veil in sunder breaks,
  The solid marbles rend.

3 'Tis done! the precious ransom's paid!
  "Receive my soul!" he cries:
  See where he bows his sacred head;
  He bows his head, and dies!

4 But soon he'll break death's envious chain,
  And in full glory shine:
  O Lamb of God, was ever pain,
  Was ever love, like thine?
  Samuel Wesley.

GROSTETE. L. M.

249 *Awake! Jerusalem, awake!*

1 Awake! Jerusalem, awake!
  No longer in thy sins lie down:
  The garment of salvation take;
  Thy beauty and thy strength put on.

2 Shake off the dust that blinds thy sight,
  And hides the promise from thine eyes;
  Arise, and struggle into light;
  The great Deliverer calls, "Arise!"

3 Shake off the bands of sad despair;
  Zion, assert thy liberty;
  Look up, thy broken heart prepare,
  And God shall set the captive free.

4 Vessels of mercy, sons of grace,
  Be purged from every sinful stain;
  Be like your Lord, his word embrace,
  Nor bear his hallowed name in vain.
  Charles Wesley.

SONGS—MISCELLANEOUS.

SILVER STREET. S. M.

250 *Met in his name.*

1 Jesus, we look to thee,
  Thy promised presence claim;
  Thou in the midst of us shalt be,
  Assembled in thy name.

2 Thy name salvation is,
  Which here we come to prove;
  Thy name is life, and health, and peace,
  And everlasting love.

3 Not in the name of pride
  Or selfishness we meet;
  From nature's paths we turn aside,
  And worldly thoughts forget.

4 We meet the grace to take,
  Which thou hast freely given;
  We meet on earth for thy dear sake,
  That we may meet in heaven.

5 Present we know thou art,
  But O thyself reveal!
  Now, Lord, let every bounding heart
  The mighty comfort feel.

6 O may thy quickening voice
  The death of sin remove;
  And bid our inmost souls rejoice,
  In hope of perfect love.
  Charles Wesley.

UXBRIDGE. L. M.

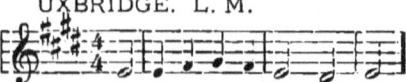

251 *Jehovah's holiness.*

1 Holy as thou, O Lord, is none;
  Thy holiness is all thine own;
  A drop of that unbounded sea
  Is ours,—a drop derived from thee:

2 And when thy purity we share,
  Thine only glory we declare;
  And, humbled into nothing, own,
  Holy and pure is God alone.

3 Sole, self-existing God and Lord,
  By all thy heavenly hosts adored,
  Let all on earth bow down to thee,
  And own thy peerless majesty.

4 Thy power unparalleled confess,
  Established on the rock of peace;
  The rock that never shall remove,
  The rock of pure, almighty love.
  Charles Wesley.

MARLOW. C. M.

252 *The kingdoms one.*

1 Happy the souls to Jesus joined,
  And saved by grace alone;
  Walking in all his ways, they find
  Their heaven on earth begun.

2 The Church triumphant in thy love,
  Their mighty joys we know:
  They sing the Lamb in hymns above,
  And we in hymns below.

3 Thee in thy glorious realm they praise
  And bow before thy throne;
  We in the kingdom of thy grace:
  The kingdoms are but one.

4 The holy to the holiest leads,
  And thence our spirits rise;
  For he that in thy statutes treads
  Shall meet thee in the skies.
  Charles Wesley.

SESSIONS. L. M.

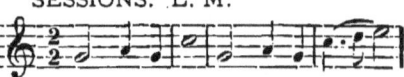

253 *For lowliness and purity.*

1 Jesus, in whom the Godhead's rays
  Beam forth with mildest majesty;
  I see thee full of truth and grace,
  And come for all I want to thee.

2 Save me from pride—the plague expel,
  Jesus, thine humble self impart:
  O let thy mind within me dwell;
  O give me lowliness of heart.

3 Enter thyself, and cast out sin;
  Thy spotless purity bestow:
  Touch me, and make the leper clean,
  Wash me, and I am white as snow.

4 Sprinkle me, Saviour, with thy blood
  And all thy gentleness is mine;
  And plunge me in the purple flood,
  Till all I am is lost in thine.
  Charles Wesley.

TOPICAL INDEX.

The figures refer to the hymns.

Affliction, 14, 100.
Anniversary, 54, 80, 232, 234, 236, 238, 240.
Assurance, 64, 77, 124, 246.
Childhood : Christ's love for, 222, 224, 225, 226, 228.
  Calling, 224, 227.
  Consecrated, 31, 219, 222.
  Giving praise, 5, 17, 67, 81, 218, 220.
  God's love for, 17, 58, 222, 226.
  Home in heaven, 58, 222.
  In temptation, 15, 142, 161, 168, 181.
  Prayer for forgiveness, 226.
  Seeking help, 7, 81, 219, 223, 225.

Christ: Advent, 48, 52, 54, 55, 63, 65-67, 69, 71, 72, 82, 84.
  Ascension, 23, 44, 49, 74, 115.
  Calling, 83, 97, 101, 105-107, 112, 121, 129-131, 134, 136, 137, 146, 190, 221, 222, 224, 227.
  Character and Attributes, 30, 65, 75, 251, 253.
  Friend of children, 5, 58, 71, 218, 222, 224, 225, 228.
  His reign, 44, 49, 59, 61, 65, 68, 80, 81, 115, 184, 188, 197, 199, 203, 234, 247.
  Redeemer and Saviour, 4-6, 13, 17, 34, 37, 41, 49, 51, 55, 59-63, 67, 71, 72, 76, 77, 81, 84, 87, 97, 98, 100, 103, 106, 111, 115, 117, 118, 124, 128, 132, 134, 136, 137, 140, 144, 150, 163, 165, 170, 171, 184, 187, 188, 191, 197, 236, 248.
  Risen, 23, 24, 47, 49, 50, 59, 61, 68, 74, 84, 115.
  Songs of, 44-87.
  Source of comfort, 6, 12, 13, 37, 51, 59, 64, 65, 69, 73, 243.
  Suffering and death, 50, 71, 73, 76, 81, 115, 248.
  Worshiped, 5, 6, 9, 12, 16, 18, 22, 30, 33, 35, 37, 40, 42, 47, 48, 51, 54, 56, 59, 61, 62, 65-69, 71, 73, 77, 84, 85, 87, 180, 185, 218, 236, 244.

Christian life: Songs of, 139-180. See also "Affliction," "Consecration," "Trust," "Providence," "Work."

Church: Fellowship, 4, 27, 28.
  Glorious, 1, 4, 27, 128, 185, 203, 239, 249.
  God in midst of, 185, 189, 249.
  Songs of, 182-191.
  Spreading the gospel, 167, 182-184, 187, 189, 203.
  Toil for, 99, 156, 192.
  Triumphant, 157, 184, 185, 189, 204, 234.

Consecration, 11, 69, 77, 79, 98, 99, 113, 123, 127, 145, 147-149, 154, 155, 166, 168, 171, 177.

God: Calling, 42, 97, 122, 131, 135.
  Creator, 6, 30, 43, 61.
  Goodness of, 29, 31, 35, 36, 41, 42, 73, 114, 180.
  Invoked, 22, 34, 37, 86.
  Praised, 3, 13, 30, 36, 41, 43, 157, 197, 218, 244.
  Songs of, 29-43.

Gratitude, 7, 29, 33, 73.

Heaven, 38, 80, 162, 169, 201.
  Songs of, 207-216.

Holy Spirit: Invoked, 19, 22, 86, 88, 89, 90.
  Songs of the, 88-91.
  Worshiped, 30, 37, 89, 218, 241, 244.

Invitation, 29, 42, 57, 97, 112, 120-122, 131.

Joy, 33, 37, 62, 75, 124, 126, 127, 163, 180, 216.
Little ones: Songs for, 217-228.
Mercy, 29, 42, 112, 122, 125, 245.
Miscellaneous, 229-253.
Missionary, 182, 184, 185, 187, 189, 190, 192, 247.
Obedience, 60, 154, 156, 190, 191, 219, 237, 345.
Peace, 8, 10, 65, 78, 173, 175.
Patriotic, 231.
Praise, 1-3, 5, 6, 16-18, 26, 28, 30, 33, 40, 49, 54, 59, 67, 69, 80, 85, 87, 111, 124, 143, 157, 173, 185, 197, 199, 241, 244, 252.
Prayer, 2, 4, 7, 8, 10, 14, 20, 32, 34, 45, 70, 78, 98, 152, 161, 178, 181, 226, 242, 245.
Promises, 38, 46, 57, 70, 141, 146, 165, 227.
Providence, 6, 7, 14, 20, 29, 35, 42.
Reward, 9, 43, 58, 70, 73, 75, 186, 187, 194, 198, 236, 239, 243.
Sabbath: Songs of the, 21-28.
Salvation: Offered, 105-108, 110-114, 120-122, 131, 139.
  Provided, 67, 72, 73, 84, 93, 97, 100, 102, 106, 110, 112, 115, 118-120, 122, 131, 133, 138.
  Sought, 98, 100, 101, 107, 110, 113, 119, 125, 137.
  Songs of, 97-138.
Scriptures, 27.
  Songs of, 92-96.
Seasons: Harvest, 241.
  Summer, 238, 240.
Supplication: For blessing, 7, 8, 13, 19, 32, 69, 86, 116, 132, 141, 226.
  Forgiveness, 4, 14, 98, 125, 226.
  Guidance, 8, 13, 14, 70, 116, 152, 161, 164, 219, 239.
  Help, 10, 13, 20, 34, 78, 105, 116, 142, 152, 161, 168, 199, 253.
  Peace, 8, 10, 14, 19, 21, 78, 100, 175, 199.
  Rest, 100, 130, 199.
  Salvation, 14, 32, 45, 105, 123, 125, 132, 152, 161, 199, 253.
Temperance, 229.
Thanksgiving, 241.
Trust: For guidance, 13, 14, 19, 51, 64, 70, 89, 100, 223, 225.
  Salvation, 2, 14, 35, 39, 45, 51, 56, 62, 64, 76-79, 100, 105, 125, 139, 147, 148, 163, 165, 176, 177, 181, 193, 250.
  In trial, 8, 13, 15, 45, 57, 89, 105, 150, 152, 181.
Warning, 101, 102, 106, 108, 110, 134, 146.
Witnessing, 150, 151, 159, 160, 172, 230.
Work, 11, 37, 53, 77, 133, 149, 151, 154, 155, 159, 160, 171, 182, 183, 187, 188, 190, 192-198, 200, 201, 203-206, 233, 237.
Worship: Morning, 22, 23, 25-27, 39.
  Evening, 15, 20, 21, 27, 39.
  Opening, 1, 2, 4, 7, 9, 17, 19, 23.
  Closing, 7, 8, 13, 19, 20, 21.
  Songs of, 1-20.
Young people's societies, 192-206.

INDEX.

TITLES AND FIRST LINES.

To facilitate the finding of Hymns the *Titles* are set in SMALL CAPS on the margin, and *First Lines* in Roman, slightly to the right.

A

	Hymn
ABBA, FATHER.............................	86
Abba, Father, hear thy child........	86
AGAIN, O'ER ALL THE CHRISTIAN EARTH...	82
A JOYFUL SONG.........................	33
ALL ARE MINE...........................	46
ALLELUIA! SWEETLY SING................	240
ALL FOR JESUS..........................	154
All for Jesus, all for Jesus..........	154
All glory to Jesus be given..........	104
All is bright and cheerful round us...	240
All the promises of Jesus............	46
ALL THE WAY............................	243
All the way the Saviour leads me.....	243
A mighty fortress is our God........	35
And can I yet delay..................	132
Angels tell the joyful story.........	85
Are you weary, are you heavy-hearted.	140
ART THOU WEARY?......................	57
Art thou weary, art thou languid.....	57
At the Lamb's high feast we sing.....	59
AUREOLA. L. M.........................	165
Awake, Jerusalem, awake.............	249
AWAKE, MY SOUL. L. M.................	6
Awake, my soul, in joyful lays.......	6

B

Beautiful country, land of light......	162
Behold the Saviour of mankind.......	248
BELMONT. C. M..........................	2
BEMERTON. C. M.........................	34
BEST OF ALL.............................	153
BE WITH ME EVERY MOMENT.............	161
BOAST NOT OF TO-MORROW..............	136
Boast not thyself of to-morrow.......	136
BOLTON. 7s, 6s.........................	241
BREAST THE WAVE, CHRISTIAN...........	174
Breast the wave, Christian, when it is strongest............................	174
BRINGING IN THE SHEAVES..............	179
BY FAITH ALONE........................	123

C

	Hymn
CALLING, PLEADING, WAITING............	106
CHILDREN OF JERUSALEM.................	220
Children of the heavenly King........	143
CHIME ON................................	27
Christians, lift your voices..........	87
Christians, lo, the fields are whit'ning..	183
Christ is knocking at my sad heart...	105
Christ, the Lord, is risen to-day......	49
Come, every soul by sin oppressed....	107
Come, Holy Spirit, come..............	88
Come, Holy Spirit, raise our songs....	90
COME, JESUS, REDEEMER.................	70
Come, Jesus, Redeemer, abide thou with me...........................	70
Come, let us use the grace divine.....	166
COME, MY SOUL, THOU MUST BE WAKING..	25
Come, sinners, to the gospel feast....	120
Come, thou long expected Jesus......	247
CONSECRATION..........................	147
CULFORD. 7s...........................	30

D

DALLAS. 7s.............................	94
DARWALL. H. M.........................	197
DELAYING TO COME......................	134
DEVIZES. C. M..........................	166
DIJON. 7s.............................	41
DIVINE UNION..........................	126
DO IT NOW..............................	196
DO SOMETHING TO-DAY..................	198
DRAW ME TO THEE......................	152

E

EARNEST WORK FOR JESUS...............	194
Eternal Father, thou hast said.......	184
EVER LOOKING UPWARD.................	145
Ever looking upward as a trusting child.............................	145

228

TITLES AND FIRST LINES.

F

	Hymn
Father, to thee my soul I lift	34
Fear not, O troubled soul, nor yield	165
FEDERAL STREET	23
FORBID THEM NOT	228
FOREVER WITH THE LORD	213
Forth in thy name, O Lord, I go	11
FORTH TO THE FIGHT	205
Forth to the fight, ye ransomed	205
FORTRESS. 8, 7, 6	35
FORWARD BE OUR WATCHWORD	204
FULLNESS OF JOY. L. M	214
Fullness of joy for evermore	214

G

GERAR. S. M	88
GIVE ME THE BIBLE. P. M	92
Give me the Bible, star of gladness	92
GIVE YE TO JEHOVAH	36
Give ye to Jehovah, O sons of the mighty	36
GLADLY WE HAIL THIS FESTAL DAY	234
GLORIA PATRI	244
GLORY BE TO GOD MOST HIGH	54
Glory be to God on high	41
Glory, glory, glory be to the Father	244
GLORY TO GOD, PEACE ON EARTH	69
GLORY TO THE FATHER GIVE	218
GOD CARETH FOR ME	43
GOD LOVED THE WORLD OF SINNERS LOST	114
GOD'S PROMISES	38
GO FORWARD, CHRISTIAN SOLDIER	206
GOING HOME AT LAST	212
GO, LABOR ON	192
Go, labor on while it is day	192
GO, TELL IT TO JESUS	150
Go, tell it to Jesus, go tell him thy woe	150
GO TELL THE WORLD OF HIS LOVE	151
GRATEFUL PRAISE	81
GREETING GLEE	232

H

Hail, holy morn, whose early ray	23
HAIL, SACRED MORN	74
Hail, sacred morn, whose golden light	74
HAIL TO THE LORD'S ANOINTED	65
HALLELUJAH! 8s and 7s	157
Hallelujah! song of gladness	157
HAMBURG. L. M	120
Happy the souls to Jesus joined	252
HARK, HARK, MY SOUL, THY FATHER'S VOICE IS CALLING	42
HARK, MY SOUL, IT IS THE LORD	97
HARK, THE VOICE OF JESUS CALLING	101
Hark, the voice of Jesus calling	190
Hark, what mean those holy voices	54
Have you had a kindness shown	230
HEAR MY PRAYER	14
Hear thou my prayer in heaven	14

	Hymn
HEART OF JESUS	45
Heart of Jesus, rent in twain	45
HEAR US, HOLY JESUS	181
HEAVENLY FATHER, GRANT THY BLESSING	7
HEAVENLY FATHER, SEND THY BLESSING	19
HEAVEN OUR HERITAGE	202
Heirs to the kingdom of Jesus the Lord	151
HE HAS COME	127
He has come, he has come	127
HELP THE ERRING	233
Help the erring, help the weary	233
Here on earth, where foes surround us	128
HERVAS. 11s, with chorus	37
HE WAS NOT WILLING	133
He was not willing that any should perish	133
Ho, every one that thirsts, draw nigh	122
Holy as thou, O Lord, is none	251
Holy Bible, book divine	94
HOLY BIBLE, WELL I LOVE THEE	95
Holy, holy, holy, Lord God of hosts	30
HOME ALL BEAUTIFUL	162
HOME TO-NIGHT	208
How can a sinner know	246
How gentle God's commands	81
How sweetly sounds the call	130
How sweet the place of prayer	4
HOW I LOVE JESUS	73
HOW TO WIN	99
HUMMEL. C. M	24

I

I AM RESTING IN THE SAVIOUR'S LOVE	163
I am safe in the Rock that is higher than I	158
I AM SHELTERED IN THEE	158
I AM THE WAY	186
I AM TRUSTING THEE, LORD JESUS	176
I BRING MY SINS TO THEE	98
I bring to thee, my Saviour	116
IF I COME TO JESUS	221
If I come to Jesus he will make me glad	221
If you feel a love for sinners	99
I have read of the sweet olden story	215
I love the name of Jesus	51
I'm a lonely traveler here	169
I'M KNEELING AT THE DOOR	125
I'm kneeling, Lord, at mercy's gate	125
"INASMUCH"	171
In from the high-ways, in from the by-ways	186
In heavenly love abiding	175
INNOCENTS. 7s	59
INVOCATION	168
In the ark most holy	79
IN THE ROSY LIGHT OF MORNING BRIGHT	17
In the Saviour's steps I'll follow	195

TITLES AND FIRST LINES.

	Hymn
I Once Was a Stranger	117
I once was a stranger to grace and to God	117
Is Your Light Shining?	188
Is your light shining brightly, my brother	188
It is from Him. L. M.	148
I Want a Heart to Pray	141
I Want to Be a Worker	201
I want to be a worker for the Lord	201
I watched the ships that come and go	202
I Will Follow Thee	109
I Will Seek the Lord To-day	137

J

Jerusalem	211
Jerusalem, my happy home	211
Jesus all my grief is sharing	153
Jesus Calling	130
Jesus Calls Thee	83
Jesus Christ is Passing By	112
Jesus, Friend of Children, Hear	225
Jesus, I come, I come for light	113
Jesus, in whom the Godhead's rays	253
Jesus is Mighty to Save	103
Jesus is our Shepherd	58
Jesus, I will follow thee	109
Jesus, let thy pitying eye	178
Jesus Lives	44
Jesus lives—no longer now	44
Jesus Only	170
Jesus only, is the motto	170
Jesus, Only Jesus	60
Jesus, Tender Shepherd	226
Jesus, tender Shepherd, hear me	226
Jesus These Eyes Have Never Seen	56
Jesus, thou everlasting King	9
Jesus, Saviour, Pilot Me	13
Jesus, we look to thee	250
Jesus, who for us didst bear	181

K

Kind Words Can Never Die	217

L

Lead Me	164
Lead me, O effulgent Light	164
Learning of Jesus	191
Learning of Jesus the lessons of truth	191
Leighton. C. M.	149
Lift Up the Gospel Banner	160
Lift up your hearts to things above	80
Light of Life	3
Light of life, seraphic fire	3
Like the prodigal of old	137
Lisbon. S. M.	132
Little One, Come to Me	227
Lischer. H. M.	22
Living for Jesus	156

	Hymn
Look Up, Lift Up	155
Look Up, Look Up to Jesus	193
Look up, look up to Jesus each day	193
Look up to Jesus, lift up thy neighbor	155
Lord, if at thy command	167
Lord, have mercy upon us, and incline our hearts	245
Lord, in the Morning Thou Shall Hear	26
Lord of the Worlds Above	1
Lord, Teach a Child to Pray	223
Lord, we come in faith believing	168
Lo, the harvest-field is bending	187
Luton. C. M.	122

M

Maidstone. 7s, D.	239
Mainzer. L. M.	16
Marching on to Zion	236
Marching to Zion	143
Mason. L. M.	90
Master, the Tempest is Raging	78
Migdol. L. M.	185
Mission Song. 8s, 7s, D	190
More of earnest work for Jesus	194
Mornington. S. M	10
My God, the spring of all my joys	180
My Native Land	231
My native land! My native land	231
My body, soul, and spirit	147

N

Neapolis, L. M.	11
Nearer the Cross	177
Nearer the cross, my heart can say	177
Noel. C. M.	180
Now Bless Me	116

O

Of him who did salvation bring	118
O glorious promises of God	38
O Guide to richest treasures	219
O home to-night, yes, home to-night	208
O how happy are they	124
Oh, the Thought that Jesus Loves Me	173
O join with the worshiping angels to sing	43
Olmutz. S. M.	31
O my heart is thrilled with joy	163
O my Saviour, how I love thee	77
Once for All the Saviour Died	115
Once in Bethlehem of Judah	71
Once when the world lay a-weary	84
One Harmonious Chorus	128
One more day is dying	135
One Sweetly Solemn Thought	209
Only Trust Him	107
On our way rejoicing	37
O sing the power of love divine	75
O sometimes the shadows are deep	139
O thou whom in ancient time	16

TITLES AND FIRST LINES.

	Hymn
OUR BLEST REDEEMER, ERE HE BREATHED.	91
OUR FATHER WATCHETH O'ER US	29
Our Father, who art in heaven	242
OUR HEAVENLY GUIDE	219
OUT ON AN OCEAN ALL BOUNDLESS WE RIDE.	210
Out on the midnight deep	152
O WE ARE VOLUNTEERS	203
O we are volunteers in the army	203
O what amazing words of grace	131
OZREM. S. M.	167

P

PASS IT ON	230
PENITENCE. 7s, 6s, 8	178
PERFECT PEACE	175
PILGRIM, WATCH AND PRAY	15
Pleasant are thy courts above	239
PLEDGE HYMN	195
PRAISE, MY SOUL, THE KING OF HEAVEN	40
PRAISE THE LORD, FOR HIS LOVE TO ME	124
PRAISE THE LORD, YE HEAVENS, ADORE HIM	18
PRAYER	12
Pray, without ceasing, pray	12
PRINCE OF PEACE	66
Prince of peace, the Lord's anointed	66
PRINCETHORPE. 6s, 5s, D	58

R

Rally for the cause of temperance	229
READY FOR LABOR	237
Ready to follow God's command	237
REFUGE	142
REJOICE AND BE GLAD	216
Rejoice and be glad, ye children of Zion	216
REJOICE, THE LORD IS KING	80
RESPONSES TO THE COMMANDMENTS	245
REX INFANS. 8s, 7s	71
ROCKPORT. 7s, 6s, 8	144
ROUND THE THRONE OF GLORY	235

S

Salvation, O the joyful sound	111
SAVIOUR, I COME TO THEE	100
SAWLEY. C. M.	32
SEE, ISRAEL'S GENTLE SHEPHERD STANDS	222
SEEK, MY SOUL	110
Seek, my soul, the narrow gate	110
SEND THE LIGHT	182
SHALL I LET HIM IN?	105
Shine on our souls, eternal God	32
SILENT NIGHT	63
Silent night, holy night	63
SING A HYMN TO JESUS	172
Sing a hymn to Jesus when the heart is faint	172
SING HIS PRAISE	5
Sing the praise of him forever	5
Sing to the Lord of harvest	241

	Hymn
SING WITH ALL THE SONS OF GLORY	47
SINNER, WHAT SAY YOU?	135
SOFTLY FADES THE TWILIGHT RAY	21
Softly on the breath of evening	15
Softly, softly, Christ is calling	227
Soldiers of Christ, a holy cause defending	236
SOLDIERS OF THE CROSS, ARISE	159
Soon may the last glad song arise	185
Sow, ere the evening falls	149
Sowing in the morning	179
STILL, STILL WITH THEE	39
Striving to do my Master's will	156
Sweet are the promises	146
SWEET IS THE WORK, O LORD	28
SWEET SAVIOUR, BLESS US ERE WE GO	20
Sweet, sweet, sweet the swell	55

T

Teach me, O Lord, by faith alone	123
TELL IT TO JESUS ALONE	140
TEMPERANCE RALLY	229
Tenderly our Father	29
THE ANGELS' STORY	85
THE BANNER OF THE CROSS	53
THE BATTLE HYMN OF MISSIONS	184
THE BETHLEHEM BABE	55
THE CHRISTIAN'S WORK SONG	183
The day of resurrection	68
The evening shades are falling	212
THE FIRST NOWELL	48
The first Nowell, the angel did say	48
The gentle winds are blowing	238
THE GREAT PHYSICIAN	138
The Great Physician now is near	138
THE JOYFUL MORN	67
The joyful morn is breaking	67
THE JOYFUL SOUND	111
THE LEAVES OF LIFE	93
The Lord, he is my strength and stay	143
The Lord of Sabbath let us praise	24
THE LORD'S PRAYER	242
THE NAME OF JESUS	51
THE PLACE OF PRAYER	4
The praying spirit breathe	10
THE PRECIOUS LOVE OF JESUS	75
THERE IS A GREEN HILL FAR AWAY	76
There is a name I love to hear	73
There is no sweeter story told	228
There is work for one and all	196
There's a call comes ringing	182
There's a rose that is blooming for you	72
There's not a ray of sunshine	129
THERE'S WORK FOR US ALL	200
There's work for us all in the labor of love	200
THE ROCK THAT IS HIGHER THAN I	139
THE ROSE OF SHARON	72
THE SAVIOUR BIDS THEE COME	129

TITLES AND FIRST LINES.

	Hymn
The Saviour Calls	108
The Saviour calls in accents clear	108
The Saviour is calling, O sinner, for thee	106
The Shadows of the Evening Hours	8
The Song of Salvation	84
The Sweet Olden Story	215
The Triumph Song	87
The Water of Life	207
The water of life, a clear crystal river	207
Thou, O sinner, art delaying	134
Thou Son of God, my inmost soul	64
Thou Who Camest from Above	89
Thou who once with man didst dwell	225
Thy sins I bore on Calvary's tree	83
'Tis So Sweet to Trust in Jesus	62
'Tis Summer Time	238
To-day He is Calling	224
To-day he is calling, his gentle voice hear	224
To-day the Saviour Calls	102
To Thee I Come	113
Truro. L. M.	9
Trusting in Jesus	64

V

Vain, delusive world, adieu............ 144

W

Ware. L. M.	118
Watchman. 7d.	189
Watchman, tell us of the night	189
We bring no glittering treasures	81

	Hymn
We Come Thy Praise to Sing	199
We come with joy to greet you here	232
We have no outward righteousness	119
Welcome, delightful morn	22
Welcome, Happy Morning	50
Welcome, happy morning, age to age shall say	50
Welcome, Jesus, Welcome	79
We leave the world of care	27
What Glory Gilds the Sacred Page	96
Whenever trials press my soul	142
When in the tempest, he'll hide me	103
When, Marshaled On the Nightly Plain	52
Where He Leads I'll Follow	146
While Jesus Whispers to You	121
Who can unfold the bliss untold	126
Who is This?	61
Who is this, a stranger lying	171
Who is this, so weak and helpless	61
Who Will Gather?	187
Winchester Old. C. M.	131
Within thy house, O Lord, Our God	2
Wolhayes. 7s.	89
Wondrous Love	77
Worgan	49

Y

Yes, I will bless thee	33
Yes, Jesus is Mighty to Save	104
Ye that love the name of Jesus	53
Ye winds that once by Chebar's flood	93
Yonder's My Home	169
Young men and maidens raise	197
You're longing to work for the Master	198

THE END.

www.ingramcontent.com/pod-product-compliance
Lightning Source LLC
Chambersburg PA
CBHW022011220426
43663CB00007B/1038